Hitler's Jewish Wife

Hitler's Jewish Wife

A Forensic Journey Into the Most Intimate Secret of the Third Reich

(Second Edition)

By Anthony Brewer

Unbound Press

Hitler's Jewish Wife: A Forensic Journey Into the Most
Intimate Secret of the Third Reich

These images remain the property of their original
copyright owners. All images used are properly credited
whenever possible. If any rights holder believes an image
has been misused, please contact jandajtk@outlook.com to
arrange proper credit or remove the image. If images are
not credited, they were created by the author using AI
assisted software. All efforts have been made to maintain
originality and avoid infringement. Disclaimers and Terms
of Use: The publisher and author do not warrant or
represent that the contents within are accurate and disclaim
all warranties and are not liable for any damages
whatsoever. Although all attempts were made to verify
information, they do not assume responsibility for errors or
omissions, and the information contained herein should not
be used as a source of legal, business, accounting, financial,
or any other professional advice.

Published by Unbound Press
ISBN (Paperback): 978-1-971207-05-6 (Second Edition)
ISBN (Hardcover): 978-1-971207-06-3 (Second Edition)
Second Edition published December 2025
First Edition published September 2025

Table of Contents

Dedication

This book is for those who know that science can rewrite not only our family stories, but the stories nations tell about themselves.

v

"There is nothing concealed that will not be disclosed, or hidden that will not be made known."

—Luke 12:2

Introduction

IN 2009, SCIENTISTS AT a small DNA testing facility analyzed a set of historical genetic samples that would unsettle long-standing assumptions about the inner circle of the Third Reich. The results did not rewrite the military history of World War II or alter the documented crimes of the Nazi regime. But they did introduce an unexpected and deeply uncomfortable contradiction—one that struck at the ideological core of Adolf Hitler's worldview.

DNA, unlike propaganda or memory, is indifferent to belief.

Political movements can manipulate narratives, regimes can suppress records, and historians can debate interpretation. But genetic material preserves information in a form that is remarkably resistant to distortion. Encoded within each person's DNA is a record of ancestral migrations and population histories—patterns modern science can now identify with increasing precision.

Eva Braun, the woman Adolf Hitler married in the final hours of his life, carried such a record.

Genetic analysis associated with Braun's remains indicated the presence of mitochondrial DNA markers commonly linked to Ashkenazi Jewish ancestry. This finding, emerging decades after her death, stood in stark contrast to the racial ideology that defined the regime she lived beside—and to the assumptions held by both Braun herself and the man she married.

Eva Braun lived and died believing she was a German Catholic woman of unremarkable lineage. Hitler died convinced that he had chosen a racially "pure" Aryan wife.

Neither could have imagined that advances in genetic science would one day complicate that certainty.

This book does not argue that Eva Braun was Jewish in any religious, cultural, or social sense. DNA cannot determine belief, identity, or lived experience. What it can do is illuminate ancestry—sometimes revealing genetic connections that family records, religious affiliation, and personal history never acknowledged or even suspected.

That distinction matters.

The Nazi racial system was built on the claim that blood determined worth, loyalty, and destiny. Yet modern genetics has shown that human populations are deeply interwoven, shaped by centuries of migration, conversion, assimilation, and survival. The very categories the regime treated as biologically absolute collapse under scientific scrutiny.

Eva Braun's genetic profile does not stand alone. As historical DNA analysis expands—examining remains, personal artifacts, and family lines long thought closed—similar contradictions continue to surface. These discoveries do not diminish historical responsibility, nor do they absolve ideology of its consequences. But they do expose the fragility of racial mythmaking and the ease with which certainty can be constructed on incomplete knowledge.

Eva Braun's story sits at the intersection of secrecy, ideology, and science. It is not a sensational footnote to history, but a case study in how modern tools can challenge long-standing assumptions—sometimes in ways that

history's architects would have found intolerable.

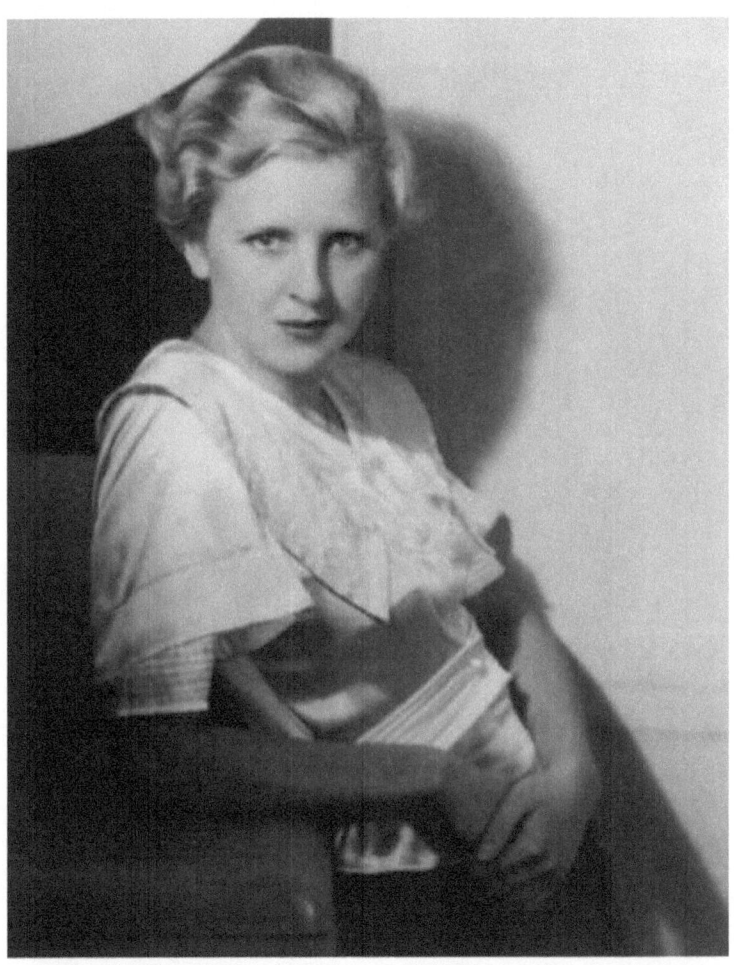

U.S. National Archives and Records Administration (NARA).
Eva Braun Photographs Collection, ca. 1930s–1940s. Washington,
D.C.

Chapter 1—The World that Made Eva Braun

———————————❖———————————

THE STORY OF EVA Braun and her hidden heritage
begins in the shattered heart of early 20th-century
Germany, a country broken by war and pulled toward a
deadly new ideology. Her life unfolds in a nation struggling
to recover from defeat, revolution, and the dangerous
promise of rebirth.

World War I and Its Aftermath (1914-1919)

When World War I ended in late 1918, Germany was
broken. Four years of brutal fighting had killed about two
million German soldiers and wrecked the economy. The
Treaty of Versailles then punished the country further:
Germany lost territory, had to pay massive reparations, and
was forced to accept the "war guilt" clause that blamed it
for starting the war. This shock and humiliation shaped the
next generation of Germans, including Adolf Hitler and
Eva Braun.

From this wreckage emerged the Weimar Republic,
Germany's first attempt at democracy. It brought new
social freedoms and a burst of art and culture, but beneath
the surface, life was unstable. The government was fragile,
and many Germans did not fully trust the new system that
had emerged from the ruins of the old empire.

Hyperinflation and fear

In 1923, disaster struck again. Hyperinflation sent prices
soaring so quickly that savings and pensions were wiped
out almost overnight. Middle-class families who had

worked hard for security watched their money turn into scraps of paper.

People came home at night only to find that a loaf of bread cost more than it had that morning. The trauma left deep anger and fear, especially among those who felt they had done everything "right" yet still lost everything.

As the country struggled to recover, the 1929 Wall Street Crash in the United States sent shock waves around the world, severely damaging Germany's fragile economy. Factories closed, banks failed, and mass unemployment spread through cities and towns.

Political street fights erupted between communist groups on one side and nationalist and right-wing militias on the other. Many ordinary Germans, tired of chaos and fear, began to crave order, stability, and a return to what they saw as "traditional values."

It was in this troubled and restless Germany that Eva Braun grew up amid a dark new power rising around her.

The Nazi Rise to Power (1920-1933)

Into this chaos stepped Adolf Hitler and his Nazi Party. The party, founded in 1920, claimed that Germany's problems came from communists, Jews, and the "November criminals" who had agreed to the surrender in World War I.

Hitler promised to restore German greatness and "racial purity" through his ideology of National Socialism. By 1932, mass unemployment and political deadlock in parliament helped make the Nazis the largest party in Germany. In January 1933, the aging President Paul von Hindenburg appointed Hitler Chancellor, and though he was deeply suspicious of him, Hindenburg believed he could be controlled.

The Third Reich Takes Shape (1933–1935)

Once in office, Hitler moved quickly to turn Germany into a dictatorship. In 1933, civil liberties such as freedom of speech, press, and assembly were suspended, and political opponents were arrested and sent to the first concentration camps. The Nazi regime also began secretly rebuilding the army and air force, directly violating the military limits set by the Treaty of Versailles.

These early years turned a fragile democracy into the core of what Hitler called the Third Reich, a state built on terror, loyalty to the Führer, and a vision of permanent war.

The Role of Women in Nazi Germany

In Nazi Germany, the ideal woman was summed up by the slogan "Kinder, Küche, Kirche" – children, kitchen, church. Women were expected to marry, have many children, and stay at home as devoted wives and mothers, not pursue careers or public power.

At the same time, modern life in cities like Munich still needed women to work in shops, offices, studios, and even some government jobs, so the official ideal often clashed with daily reality.

Eva Braun herself stood at the center of this contradiction. In public, she seemed to fit the obedient and feminine image the regime praised. In private, she carved out a more independent life through her photography work, her friendships, and her tastes in fashion, movies, and travel, even as she remained bound to Hitler and the narrow world around him.

Poster from the Nazi magazine Neues Volk ("A New People") issued by the Nazi Party Office of Racial Policy; by Ludwig Hohlwein 1937; picture showing the idealized German family as the core of the "Volksgemeinschaft", a pure "Aryan" family (a blond father, mother, and young child), and a flying eagle in the background.

Eva Braun: Her Early Life

Eva Anna Paula Braun was born on February 6, 1912, in Munich, Bavaria, Germany. Her father, Friedrich "Fritz" Braun, was a schoolteacher and later a headmaster; her mother, Franziska "Fanny" Kronberger Braun, was a homemaker known for her warmth and deep Catholic faith. The Braun household reflected the rhythms and values of respectable middle-class Munich—orderly, disciplined, and shaped by the expectations of bourgeois Catholic life.

Fritz Braun was a man whose identity was anchored in duty. Born in 1879 to a lower-middle-class Catholic family, he had advanced through Germany's teacher-training system by diligence rather than privilege. He carried himself with the reserve of someone who had earned his place and intended to defend it. Former pupils recalled his precise handwriting, clipped speech, and insistence on proper grammar. At home, punctual meals and correct language were nonnegotiable, and lapses were corrected without humor.

A veteran of the First World War, Fritz retained a soldier's posture long after the armistice. Yet despite his conservatism, he never embraced National Socialism. He regarded Hitler with suspicion from the outset and recoiled from the emotional excesses of the Nazi movement as it took root in Munich. When colleagues joined Nazi teachers' organizations in the 1930s, Fritz quietly refused, a decision that cost him advancement.

Respectability mattered to him; fanaticism did not. He chose to keep his classroom and his conscience separate from political spectacle. Over time, however, as the regime tightened its grip and membership became a path to security and respectability, Fritz eventually applied for and received a Party card, accepting the practical benefits that came with it even though he was never a true believer.

Eva's mother, Franziska Kronberger Braun, known to everyone as Fanny, provided the counterbalance. Born in 1885 to a family of artisans, she had worked as a seamstress before marriage and retained the easy warmth of her social background. Where Fritz emphasized discipline, Fanny offered reassurance. She was devoutly Catholic, attending Mass regularly and keeping saints' cards tucked in her prayer book, but her faith expressed itself more in kindness than in rigidity.

Within the home, she softened the strictures imposed by her husband. She allowed her daughters later bedtimes, encouraged an interest in fashion and photography, and defended small expressions of independence that Fritz viewed with concern. "Girls should have light in their lives," she insisted, a philosophy that created space for affection and emotional ease beneath the household's emphasis on outward propriety.

Biographer Angela Lambert later described Fanny Braun as "the emotional core of a home that prized outward normality above all else." That normality—carefully maintained, quietly guarded—would shape Eva Braun's understanding of the world long before Adolf Hitler entered her life.

A Bavarian Household

The Braun home in Munich reflected the quiet contradictions of middle-class Germany in the 1920s: discipline and indulgence, faith and modernity, restraint tempered by small freedoms. Fritz Braun's insistence on propriety coexisted uneasily with Fanny's belief that joy itself was not a moral failing.

The Braun Family

The Brauns had three daughters. Ilse, the eldest, composed and reliable, worked as a medical secretary and often acted as an intermediary when her father's rigidity clashed with her younger sisters' liveliness. Eva, born in 1912, was energetic, expressive, and keenly aware of herself, occupying the middle ground.

Gretl, the youngest, adored Eva and mirrored her fascination with laughter, lipstick, and dancing. The sisters were close yet competitive, each attuned to appearance and approval in her own way. Eva and Gretl shared a bond that would last into adulthood, when Gretl followed Eva into Hitler's orbit and married SS officer Hermann Fegelein.

From an early age, Eva stood out with her vitality. She enjoyed swimming, dancing, and posing for photographs, all early signs of a lifelong interest in image and self-presentation. She navigated easily between her father's demand for discipline and her mother's gentler permissiveness, internalizing both the desire to please and the longing to be seen.

Within this household of order and indulgence, Eva's character took shape. She inherited her father's sensitivity to approval and her mother's romantic softness, a combination that fostered both compliance and quiet rebellion.

She attended a convent school and received a Catholic education that emphasized moral discipline, obedience, and feminine virtue—qualities later praised by Nazi ideology as evidence of superior racial stock. Teachers remembered her as friendly and well-behaved, showing none of the supposed "foreignness" or moral deviation that Nazi theorists linked to Jewish ancestry. She was unremarkable in class, better at sports than at Latin, charming rather than scholarly.[1]

Beneath her playful exterior, there was a need to be noticed. When she left the convent-run business school at seventeen to work at a Munich photography studio, her parents approved, though with some hesitation. The job was respectable, but they worried about appearances. They never could have imagined that the man Eva would soon meet through the studio—a polite, middle-aged political figure in a dark overcoat—would change her life and connect the quiet Braun household to one of history's most infamous names.

A Fateful Encounter at the Studio on Schellingstraße

When Eva Braun walked into Heinrich Hoffmann's photographic studio on Schellingstraße for the first time in 1929, she stepped into a world of polished glass and the hum of commerce. The shop occupied a bright corner near the Odeonsplatz, a lively quarter surrounded by cafés and government offices. Inside, the air carried the sharp scent of chemical developer and floor wax. Brass lamps reflected the framed portraits lining the walls of generals, actresses, civic officials, and increasingly, the stern face of a rising politician: Adolf Hitler.

Eva was hired as a sales clerk and assistant, a modest but respectable position for a young woman of her background. Her duties were routine: greeting customers, recording orders, trimming and mounting photographs, wrapping prints in tissue paper, and balancing the cash ledger at day's end. She learned to mix developing solutions and file negatives in narrow drawers that smelled faintly of vinegar and silver nitrate.

On busy days, she swept the floor and carried trays of prints up the narrow staircase to the retouching room, where cigarette smoke hung in the air and conversation never quite stopped.

Hoffmann himself was gregarious, portly, and tireless, a man always on the move. His studio functioned as both a business and a social hub, drawing journalists, actors, and party officials who came as much to talk as to be photographed. Assistants moved briskly through the space, balancing portfolios; the click of the camera shutter punctuated the day.

Eva adapted quickly. She had an instinctive sense of

proportion and presentation, and her bright, open manner made her popular with customers. Occasionally, she posed for demonstration shots—lighting tests, new film stock, sample portraits for the window display. Though not a professional model, she photographed well: clear skin, wide eyes, and a casual vitality that felt modern. Hoffmann called her "mein kleines Fräulein Braun (my little Miss Braun)," half affection, half amusement.

Her days followed a steady rhythm. She biked through the cool morning streets, skirt hem pinned to avoid the spokes, unlocked the shop at eight, and swept the front room before customers arrived. Mornings were reserved for sittings—passport photos, brides in white lace, officers in uniform. Afternoons were spent logging invoices and retouching prints under a green-shaded lamp until evening.

For Eva, the studio was more than just a job; it was a glimpse into a bigger world. Through Hoffmann's lens, she observed the city's influential and glamorous faces, which she recognized from magazines and newspaper columns. The glossy portraits drying on the racks portrayed lives far different from her own, lives driven by attention and power.

It was there, amid the smell of developer and the hum of conversation, that she first heard Adolf Hitler's name spoken with reverence. Hoffmann, already his official photographer and an early Nazi Party member, often shared stories from rallies, describing Hitler as a man destined for leadership. Eva listened with mild curiosity, imagining not politics but prominence. When Hitler himself began visiting the studio, the atmosphere shifted. Conversations softened, movements quickened, and instructions were whispered. Everyone stood a little straighter.

To the seventeen-year-old assistant, those visits carried a quiet thrill. She might glimpse him through the darkroom door or pass him an envelope of prints. There was nothing romantic yet—only the unsettling gravity of someone who seemed to command attention without effort. The ordinary rhythms of the studio shifted in his presence.

The First Conversation

One afternoon in 1929, Adolf Hitler arrived at the studio, and Eva was sent out to fetch beer and Bavarian meatloaf for the guest. When she returned, she spoke her first words to him: Guten Appetit—"Enjoy your meal."[2] Then she blushed.

After that, she became acutely aware of his visits. He often arrived with Hoffmann or party aides to review negatives or select publicity images. He spoke sparingly, but when he did, his voice was calm, deliberate, and assured. He talked of architecture, Germany's renewal, and the importance of beauty and order. It felt less like conversation than performance, and Eva, standing behind the counter with her ledger and careful handwriting, became part of the audience.

Shadows of Fascination

Over the following year, Munich itself seemed to vibrate with change. Walking through the streets, swastika flags, Nazi posters, and marching uniforms become part of the city's background, even as women like her still went to studios, shops, and cinemas, trying to live ordinary lives inside an increasingly unordinary state. Brown-shirted men marched through the streets, flags unfurled from buildings, speeches spilled from beer halls. Hitler's name appeared daily in the newspapers.

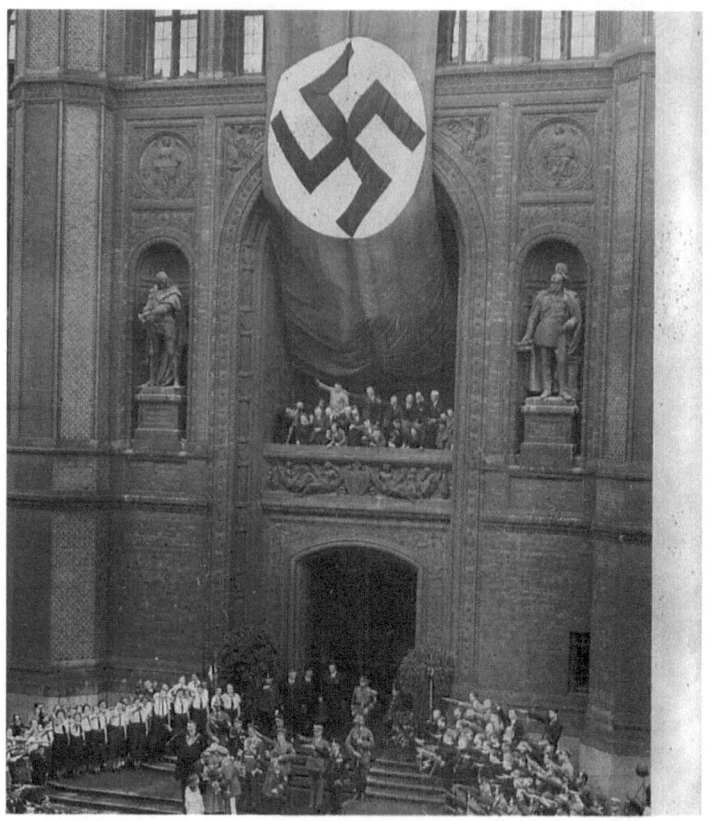

Berlin, Nazi Germany, April 10, 1935. Public Domain.

When Eva passed his posters on her way to work, she felt a private thrill, as if she shared in the world they promised. She began to imagine that he noticed her, that she was more than a shop assistant in the background of his rise. Beneath his controlled exterior, she sensed possibility—affection, perhaps even destiny.

For Eva Braun, restless and longing for significance, the studio on Schellingstraße had become the place where the familiar world quietly gave way to something far more dangerous.

A Dangerous Kind of Dream

In *Hitler Was My Friend* (1955), Heinrich Hoffmann recalled that Hitler "paid her a quiet attention." He brought small gifts, arranged occasional outings to the cinema, and took her to dinner at the Osteria Bavaria, a favored meeting place of his inner circle in Munich. Hoffmann's wife, as well as Henriette von Schirach, later confirmed that by 1931 or 1932, Hitler's interest in Eva Braun was visible, though always restrained and discreet.

"He would sometimes send her flowers, or take her to the pictures," one observer recalled. "It was innocent enough at first, but she was flattered by his interest."

Within Hoffmann's circle, the nature of the relationship was understood. Hitler used carefully measured gestures— flowers, dinners, fleeting attention—to draw Eva closer while maintaining control over the pace, the secrecy, and the terms of their connection.

For Eva, however, the arrangement was intolerably uneven.

She was never permitted access to his political world. Weeks could pass without a word from him. When he returned, it was entirely on his terms. The sudden reappearance of attention restored her sense of meaning; his absence plunged her into despair. She could not yet see that this pattern—distance followed by reward, invisibility punctuated by brief affirmation—was shaping her emotional life.

In the summer of 1932, overwhelmed by his indifference, Eva shot herself in the chest with her father's pistol. The wound was serious but not fatal. Hitler's response was measured rather than emotional. He visited her during her recovery, brought gifts, and arranged for her to move into a new apartment.

From that point forward, he kept her closer—but only within the confines of his private life. She was never acknowledged publicly, never presented as a companion, only supported quietly and kept out of sight.

For several years, Eva remained one of several women in Hitler's orbit. As his political power grew, so did the imbalance. When he vanished for long stretches, she sank into gloom. When he returned, her world brightened again. She could not yet recognize that this cycle would define her adult existence.

Outside the studio, Munich was filled with banners, marches, and speeches. Inside, Eva Braun dusted frames, balanced ledgers, and dreamed of the man who promised to restore Germany's greatness—while keeping her carefully separated from it.

Yet Eva wanted more. Over time, she learned to maneuver within the narrow space available to her. If she could not enter his public life, she would secure her place in his private one.

By 1933, Hitler had become Chancellor of Germany. His cultivated image as the unmarried "savior of the nation" was central to Nazi mythmaking; romance or marriage would have weakened the cult of devotion he and Joseph Goebbels were constructing. Eva was therefore removed almost entirely from view.

Hitler arranged for her to live first at 12 Waterloostrasse, later at 16 Prinzregentenplatz in Munich. Her expenses were paid discreetly through Hoffmann's accounts. She lived alone, occasionally visited by her sister Gretl or by Hitler's adjutants, who acted as intermediaries.

Letters from this period reveal long hours of boredom and longing—days spent waiting by the telephone, evenings prepared with care for visits that rarely came.

In 1934, the isolation intensified. As Hitler focused on consolidating power—culminating in the Night of the Long Knives—Eva remained entirely excluded. That year, she attempted suicide again, this time by overdosing on sleeping pills. Once more, she survived. Once more, Hitler drew her closer afterward. He purchased clothes and jewelry, reassured her of his affection, and began bringing her to his mountain retreat near Berchtesgaden.

By 1935, the Obersalzberg had been transformed into the Berghof, a grand alpine residence. Eva was given her own suite—near his, but not beside it. There, she constructed a private world of photographs, diary entries, and carefully staged moments, a life shaped by waiting and imagination.

The young woman who once longed simply to be noticed had stepped fully into history's shadow—unaware that she would later be remembered less for who she was than for her proximity to a man who never allowed her to be fully seen.

Eva Braun, National Archives, Public Domain

The Berghof overlooking the Obersalzberg. Hitler's private retreat and setting for political meetings with Nazi leaders and foreign dignitaries.

[1] Hoffmann, Heinrich. Hitler Was My Friend. London: Burke, 1955, p 234–37

[2] Ibid.

Chapter 2 - The Shadow of a Dictator

———————————◆———————————

ADOLF HITLER'S HATRED OF Jews was not merely political strategy or rhetorical excess. It was the foundation of a worldview built on blood, inheritance, and exclusion— a belief system that treated ancestry as destiny and framed history as a biological struggle. In Hitler's imagination, Jewish people were not simply a religious or cultural group but a contaminant, a hidden threat carried in bloodlines and passed silently from generation to generation.

This fixation made race—not citizenship, faith, or loyalty—the central measure of human worth.

Understanding Hitler's ideology requires looking beyond speeches and mass rallies to the private logic that shaped his most intimate fears. His obsession was personal, sexual, and genealogical. He believed the future of civilization depended on controlling reproduction, regulating marriage, and preventing what he described as the "corruption" of German blood.

The irony was profound. The man who would later marry Eva Braun spent decades constructing an ideology that, had it been applied honestly to his own household, would have condemned his wife by the standards he himself enforced.

A Doctrine of Blood

Hitler's antisemitism developed over years of frustration, resentment, and exposure to the racial theories circulating in Austria and Germany in the early twentieth century. As a struggling artist in Vienna, he absorbed the rhetoric of demagogues such as Karl Lueger, who blamed Jews for

21

social unrest, economic instability, and cultural decline.[1] These ideas offered Hitler something he desperately needed: a single, all-encompassing explanation for his failures.

Dr. KARL LUEGER
Bürgermeister der k. k. Reichshaupt- und Residenzstadt Wien.

Karl Lueger, Public Domain

In this worldview, complexity disappeared. Capitalism, communism, moral change, and political defeat could all be attributed to Jewish influence. The theory was total. It required no evidence beyond belief and no solution beyond removal.

What distinguished Hitler was not the originality of these ideas, but the intensity with which he fused them to a vision of biological destiny. He did not simply hate Jews; he believed they represented an existential threat embedded in bloodlines themselves. In his thinking, race was not symbolic. It was hereditary, permanent, and inescapable.

Once in power, Hitler translated obsession into policy. Hatred became law. Ideology became administration.

Marriage as a Political Risk

Nowhere was this fixation more visible than in Nazi racial legislation. The Nuremberg Laws of 1935 did more than strip Jewish citizens of rights. They attempted to regulate intimacy itself. The Law for the Protection of German Blood and German Honor criminalized marriages and sexual relationships between Jews and Germans, declaring such unions acts of Rassenschande—racial defilement.

Marriage was no longer a private decision. It was a biological threat.

Under the new system, identity was determined not by belief or behavior but by ancestry. Officials traced family lines back generations, examining baptismal records, marriage certificates, and civil documents to determine racial classification. A single Jewish grandparent could alter a person's legal status. Faith, conversion, and cultural life were irrelevant. Blood alone mattered.

Associated Press (Louis P. Lochner). "Germany Makes Drastic Rules Governing Jews." U.S. newspaper, September 16, 1935.

The system created categories—Juden, Mischlinge, "Aryans"—each with its own restrictions. The logic was relentless. If Jewishness resided in blood, it could be hidden, passed unknowingly, and discovered only through scrutiny. The danger was invisible.

There were no formal exemptions. The laws applied universally, at least in theory. Even high-ranking Nazis were subject to investigation if questions arose about ancestry or relationships. Public purity demanded private compliance.

And yet, the regime's leaders lived with constant fear of exposure.

Secrecy and Hypocrisy

The emphasis on bloodlines created a paradox at the heart of Nazi power. The more the regime obsessed over racial purity, the more vulnerable it became to what it could not fully control: genealogy itself.

Hitler understood this risk intuitively. His personal life was guarded with extraordinary care. Romance was concealed. Marriage was postponed. Women were kept out of view, not only to preserve his public image as the selfless "savior of the nation," but because intimacy itself posed danger.

The regime that demanded exhaustive genealogical proof from millions relied on secrecy to protect its own leadership from similar scrutiny.

This contradiction was never acknowledged publicly, but it shaped behavior at the highest levels. Blood was exalted, yet bloodlines were rarely examined where power was concerned. Purity was preached, while private lives were hidden behind layers of silence, intermediaries, and discretion.

The Fragility of Racial Certainty

The Nazi racial system rested on a flawed, fundamental assumption: that ancestry could be known with certainty and controlled by law. In practice, it relied on incomplete records, inconsistent documentation, and human judgment. It was a system obsessed with precision yet riddled with blind spots.

The ideology that claimed to identify contamination at a glance could not account for what lay hidden in genetic inheritance. Conversion, migration, intermarriage, and history itself had already rendered racial boundaries porous long before the Nazis tried to seal them with law.

Hitler never questioned whether the bloodlines closest to him might complicate his theories. He believed in purity because he needed to. The alternative—that identity was complex, inherited unpredictably, and resistant to ideological control—would have undermined everything he stood for.

The shadow that followed him was not merely moral hypocrisy. It was an epistemological failure: the belief that blood could be known without ever truly being examined.

Science as Alibi

Nazi racial ideology did not rely on propaganda alone. It cloaked itself in the language of science, presenting persecution as reasoned policy rather than fanatic belief. The regime understood that modern authority required more than slogans; it required the appearance of empirical legitimacy.

Race was framed as biology, not culture. Humanity, Nazi theorists claimed, could be divided into discrete hereditary groups, locked in permanent struggle. "Aryans" occupied the highest rung, and Jews were a biological threat to that supremacy.

To support this fiction, the state funded an elaborate apparatus of racial research. Physical anthropologists measured skulls, noses, and facial angles. Photographs and charts were compiled to suggest immutable differences where none existed.[2] Blood typing was pressed into service as evidence of racial hierarchy, despite the absence of any scientific basis for such conclusions. Certain blood groups were declared markers of fitness; others, signs of degeneration.[3]

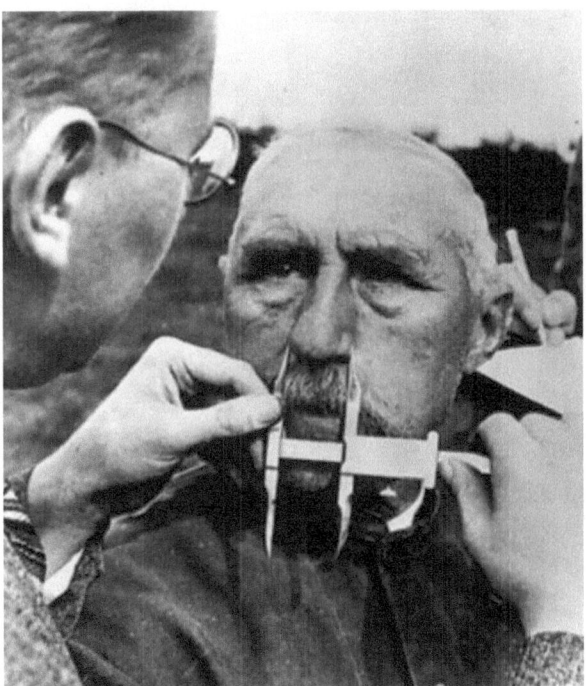

Photo of Eugenics, Public Domain

These practices borrowed the vocabulary of heredity and evolution while discarding their substance. Legitimate scientific concepts of natural selection, inheritance, and population variation were distorted into rigid hierarchies.

University professors and physicians published papers and taught courses that transformed ideology into apparent natural law. International scholarly forums, slow to recognize the danger, initially gave some of this work a platform, lending it a veneer of respectability.

The result was a system that treated extermination as something inevitable, even natural. Nazi thinkers claimed that "racial struggle" was an evolutionary law and that removing so-called inferior groups was a form of biological hygiene, not mass murder. Violence was dressed up as science, presented as clinical necessity rather than deliberate cruelty.

Yet the ideology that demanded proof of purity from millions never submitted itself to the same testing. The "science" it invoked could not survive honest investigation. When real genetic analysis finally became possible decades later, it exposed how fragile those claims had always been and how completely the Nazis' certainty collapsed under genuine scrutiny

Eva Braun, from Eva Braun's personal photo albums, now held in the U.S. National Archives and Records Administration (NARA).. Public domain.

[1] Herf, Jeffrey. The Jewish Enemy: Nazi Propaganda during World War II and the Holocaust. Cambridge, MA: Harvard University Press, 2006.

[2] Proctor, Robert N. Racial Hygiene: Medicine Under the Nazis. Cambridge, MA: Harvard University Press, 1988.

[3] Friedlander, Henry. The Origins of Nazi Genocide: From Euthanasia to the Final Solution. Chapel Hill: University of North Carolina Press, 1995.

Chapter 3—Final Vows

———————————❖———————————

FROM 1935 TO 1945, Eva Braun lived at the edge of Nazi power—close enough to benefit from it yet insulated from public scrutiny and the full reality of the regime's actions.

Her life unfolded inside a bubble of routine and privilege. She hosted gatherings, practiced photography, and filmed home movies at the mountain retreats that later became iconic symbols of the regime's private life. Servants prepared meals. Schedules revolved around leisure, shopping, and social visits. The setting was orderly, comfortable, and deliberately apolitical.

The comforts surrounding her were not neutral. The art decorating her rooms had been seized from Jewish families. The jewelry and clothing she wore were purchased with funds extracted from confiscated businesses. The labor sustaining these residences increasingly came from forced and enslaved workers. Yet within the boundaries of Hitler's private world, these realities remained abstract and unacknowledged.

A typical day might begin at the Berghof, Hitler's Alpine retreat in the Bavarian Alps. There, she woke to sweeping mountain views, ate meals prepared by staff, planned outings, and tended to her photography. The mountain air, the ordered interiors, and the rituals of domestic life created an illusion of stability.[1]

The contrast between Eva Braun's existence and that of Jewish women under Nazi rule could not have been sharper. While she shopped for luxury goods, Jewish women were stripped of property and confined to ghettos.

While she attended dinners and social gatherings, Jewish families were deported to camps.

Eva continued to remain unseen by the public that idolized Hitler, suspended between extraordinary privilege and deliberate invisibility. An invisibility that served a purpose.

If Eva Braun had been publicly acknowledged as Hitler's companion, her ancestry would have been subjected to the most exhaustive genealogical scrutiny the regime could muster. Investigators would have traced her lineage across generations, examining church registers, civil records, and family files for any indication of Jewish descent. Such investigations were routine for those seeking proximity to power.

Her employment at Heinrich Hoffmann's photography studio reinforced this assumption. Hoffmann would have been fully aware of the racial expectations governing access to the Führer, and Eva's presence there marked her as acceptable under the regime's standards.

Even so, Eva did undergo conventional genealogical screening, and nothing in those records raised alarms. On paper, her background aligned seamlessly with Nazi ideals. Her father's position as a schoolteacher and headmaster signaled discipline and civic virtue. Her mother appeared to come from a well-established Bavarian Catholic family. The records told a reassuring story.

She passed every test that could be administered using the tools of her day. What they could not reveal was what lay beyond documentation.

Eva's proximity to power gave her a vantage few possessed, yet she remained largely disengaged from politics. Her focus was on relationships and personal stability rather than ideology or consequences. She attended gatherings where genocide was discussed as policy, dined in homes where mass murder was planned, and maintained friendships with those responsible—all while preserving emotional distance from the crimes themselves.

Her social circle mirrored her isolation. Wives and girlfriends of Nazi leaders formed a parallel world devoted to fashion, leisure, and status. Together, they constructed a version of normal life that existed alongside atrocity, sustained by avoidance and silence.

The psychological mechanisms Eva relied upon—compartmentalization, rationalization, and willful blindness—were not unique. They were the same mechanisms that allowed millions of ordinary Germans to benefit from Nazi policies while denying responsibility for their consequences.

Her photography offers the clearest record of this division. Her images captured smiling officials, mountain landscapes, and intimate domestic scenes. They documented comfort and companionship, never deportations or camps, never the machinery of destruction that made such comfort possible.

As Hitler was stripping Jews of citizenship, racial scientists were developing methods to "detect" Jewish heritage, and SS officers were deporting Jewish families to death camps, Eva lived comfortably in Hitler's private residences, unaware that her genetic past carried a secret.

Final Days

As the war dragged into its final months, the grand illusions of the Third Reich fell apart on every front. In the east, the Red Army pushed relentlessly toward Germany, smashing through cities and leaving no doubt that Soviet troops would soon reach Berlin.

United States Holocaust Memorial Museum, Photograph Archives. Originally from Eva Braun's personal photo albums seized by the U.S. Army and now held by the U.S. National Archives and Records Administration (NARA). Public domain.

In the west, British and American forces crossed the Rhine and moved deeper into German territory, uncovering concentration camps and the full scale of Nazi crimes as they advanced. German cities lay in ruins from years of bombing, supply lines were collapsing, and even devoted followers could see that Hitler's promises of victory no longer matched reality.

Inside Germany, the mood shifted from fanatical hope to

fear and exhaustion. Food and fuel grew scarce, families fled in chaos, and rumors of atrocities and coming revenge spread from village to village. Officers plotted against Hitler, some attempting assassinations, while others simply tried to save what they could of their troops.

In this atmosphere of encirclement and betrayal, Hitler withdrew further into his underground headquarters, blaming generals, Jews, and entire populations for the disaster, even as his armies disintegrated around him. It was in this tightening circle of defeat that the private world he had so carefully controlled began its final collapse inward.

Soviet shells shook the bunker day and night, sending dust and concrete splinters raining from the ceiling as explosions crashed overhead. The once-carefully guarded nerve center of the Reich had become a trembling shelter, its corridors lit by dim bulbs while the world above ground was pounded into rubble.

On April 29, 1945, deep inside the shattered Führerbunker, as the Third Reich disintegrated around them, Adolf Hitler and Eva Braun were married in a brief civil ceremony.

The marriage was a decision Hitler made only when defeat was inevitable. For years, he had kept Eva Braun hidden, preserving the fiction of personal sacrifice and political purity. With Berlin collapsing and no future left to manage, secrecy no longer served its purpose. In his final hours, he finally acknowledged her role in his life.

A city official, Walter Wagner, risked his life to reach the Führerbunker amid artillery fire and Soviet patrols. The ceremony he conducted lasted barely ten minutes. Joseph

Goebbels and Martin Bormann served as witnesses. There was no religious blessing, celebration, or recognition beyond the signatures on a single document. Eva Braun became Frau Hitler for less than a day.

U.S. National Archives and Records Administration (NARA), Record Group 111-SC (Signal Corps Photographs). Ruins of Hitler's Berghof, Berchtesgaden, Germany, 1945. Public domain.

The marriage certificate itself stands as an artifact of contradiction. The regime Hitler built outlawed marriages deemed racially unacceptable, criminalizing intimacy in the name of biological purity. Yet in his final act of personal sovereignty, Hitler unknowingly defied the ideological system he had imposed on millions. Neither Hitler nor Eva knew that the union carried a deeper irony.

As they exchanged vows underground, Allied forces were liberating camps, uncovering mass graves, and

documenting the consequences of Nazi racial policy.
Within twenty-four hours, both the bride and the groom
would be dead. Within days, occupation authorities would
dismantle the regime's racial laws. The legal fiction of
purity collapsed almost as quickly as the Reich itself.

Eva Braun's transformation—from concealed
companion to acknowledged wife—came too late to change
her fate. But it crystallized the contradictions that defined
the Nazi racial state. In its final hours, it revealed what it
had always been: an ideology obsessed with blood yet
incapable of truly knowing it.

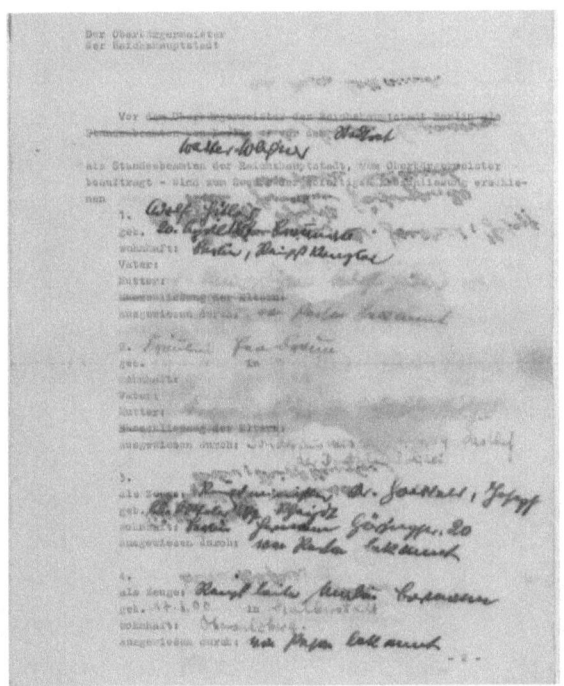

U.S. National Archives and Records Administration (NARA), Captured
German Records Collection. Marriage Certificate of Adolf Hitler and
Eva Braun, April 29, 1945. Public domain.

Death and the Clues Left Behind

On April 30, 1945, one day after the wedding, the newlyweds shared a final meal of spaghetti with tomato sauce. Eva ate little. When they finished, they withdrew into a private room and closed the door.

A shot was heard.

Rochus Misch, Hitler's bodyguard, later recalled opening the door and finding Hitler slumped by the table. Eva lay beside him on the sofa, her knees drawn up, dressed in a white-and-blue blouse with a small collar. Hitler had shot himself. Eva had taken cyanide.[2]

Eva Braun died less than twenty-four hours after becoming Hitler's wife. He had carefully planned the suicides. In his mind, capture meant humiliation and exploitation. Death was his final act of control.

Eva's decision to die with him was her final act of loyalty in a relationship that had consumed her autonomy and identity. She was not a political figure of consequence; escape may have been possible. She chose not to take it. Instead, she bound her fate to his, completing a life defined by secrecy and dependence.

Yet death did not erase everything.

Fragments remained. Strands of hair. Fibers from clothing. Objects handled, worn, or stored nearby. Collected by Allied forces and cataloged as evidence or war trophies, these remnants were boxed and archived. For decades, they lay dormant—silent witnesses to a life defined by concealment.

The regime that sought to control bloodlines had destroyed documents, burned bodies, and scattered ashes.

But it could not erase biology itself. The clues to Eva Braun's ancestry survived in forms too small to matter at the time, waiting for tools that did not yet exist.

In the end, the final secrecy failed. What ideology could not admit, science would eventually reveal.

[1] Heike B. Görtemaker, Eva Braun: Life with Hitler, trans. Damion Searls (New York: Alfred A. Knopf, 2011); United States Holocaust Memorial Museum, "Eva Braun & family vacation; Hitler at Berghof," Holocaust Survivors and Victims Resource Center Collections, accessed December 19, 2025, which documents leisure life filmed by Braun at Hitler's mountain residence; Bee Wilson, "I and My Wife: Eva Braun," London Review of Books 34, no. 1 (January 5, 2012)
[2] Rochus Misch, Hitler's Last Witness: The Memoirs of Hitler's Bodyguard (Brunswick, VIC: Scribe, 2014), chap. 14 ("Hitler's Last Day: 30 April 1945"); William J. Kole, "Hitler's Final Days Described by Bodyguard," Los Angeles Times, April 24, 2005; Matt Schudel, "Rochus Misch, Hitler's Bodyguard, Dies," Washington Post, September 6, 2013.

Chapter 4—The Hairbrush

———————————❖———————————

THE WOODEN HAIRBRUSH, ENGRAVED with the initials "E.B.," appeared unremarkable when it was recovered from Eva Braun's private apartment at the Berghof in May 1945. Elegant, well-made, and clearly personal, it looked like one more relic of a vanished private life—an object preserved for its association rather than its substance.

The Allied soldiers cataloging the contents of Hitler's mountain retreat could not have known that the brush would one day play a role in one of the most unexpected intersections of history and genetics. At the time, it was simply evidence—one item among thousands collected from the homes of the Nazi elite.

Only decades later would its significance become clear.

The Search at the Berghof: May 1945

When American forces reached Berchtesgaden in early May 1945, the Third Reich had already collapsed. Hitler was dead in Berlin, Germany had effectively surrendered, and the war in Europe was drawing to a close. Yet the Berghof—Hitler's alpine residence overlooking the Obersalzberg—remained intact enough to warrant immediate attention.

The Allied soldiers were there to collect and catalogue personal effects from the residences of Nazi leaders—items that might someday be helpful for intelligence purposes or war-crimes investigations.

US soldiers from the 101st Airborne Division pose for a photograph in Berchtesgaden, Germany, accessed October 2025.

The site was more than a private home. It had functioned as a center of informal power, a place where decisions were shaped, relationships maintained, and loyalty rewarded. Its rooms promised insight into the private world of the regime's leadership.

Elements of the U.S. 3rd Infantry Division and the 101st Airborne Division secured the area in early May. Accompanying them were specialists from the Army Counter-Intelligence Corps (CIC) and the Office of Strategic Services (OSS), tasked with gathering material that might serve intelligence, legal, and historical purposes.[1]

Intelligence, Evidence, and Intent

The Allied searches followed three primary objectives.

First, investigators sought documentary and personal evidence that could support future war crimes prosecutions: correspondence, diaries, financial records, photographs, and official papers.

Second, they aimed to recover stolen cultural property. Bavaria and neighboring regions had become repositories for looted art and artifacts seized across Europe, much of it earmarked for Hitler's planned museum in Linz.

Third, intelligence officers sought insight into the psychology of Nazi leadership. The private possessions of those at the top—their habits, tastes, and domestic environments—were treated as potential clues to how mass murder had been normalized within everyday life.

For the OSS, such details fed into the wartime effort known as the "Hitler Source Book Project," a compilation of psychological and sociological profiles of top Nazis. Personal artifacts — from Hitler's medicine bottles to Eva Braun's clothing — were viewed as clues to personality.

The Teams on the Mountain

The Royal Air Force had bombed the Berghof on April 25, 1945, leaving much of the structure damaged but not destroyed. When American forces arrived, the façade was blackened and portions of the interior burned, but basements, guesthouses, and adjacent residences remained largely intact.

Among the first officers on site were Lieutenant Colonel Robert E. G. Hall of the 101st Airborne Division, Major Floyd P. Doran of the Counter-Intelligence Corps in Berchtesgaden, and Lieutenant Colonel B. D. Taylor of the 3rd Infantry Division. They were joined by personnel from Army intelligence (G-2) and the Monuments, Fine Arts, and Archives section—the "Monuments Men"—who were charged with identifying and securing cultural property.[2]

This specialized team was trained to identify and preserve materials whose importance might not be immediately obvious—such as documents, photographs, clothing, and personal items that could contain fingerprints, handwriting, or other evidence. Intelligence officers knew they were recording an unprecedented regime, and even seemingly insignificant items could potentially yield vital information someday.

Anything found belonging to Hitler, Göring, Goebbels, Himmler, and Eva Braun was cataloged and preserved.

What They Found

Inside the Berghof and Eva Braun's adjacent apartment, investigators encountered rooms that seemed suspended in time. Wardrobes of dresses and shoes. Bottles of perfume. Jewelry cases. Photographic equipment and reels of color film documenting years of domestic life at the Obersalzberg.

Thousands of photographs and home movies—many taken by Eva herself—were later used by Allied historians to reconstruct the private routines of Hitler's circle. Albums showed holidays, visits by foreign dignitaries, and moments of staged intimacy that contrasted sharply with the regime's public image.

Eva Braun, 1930s. Public Domain.

Hitler's library and medical cabinet, along with personal stationery, uniforms, and signed portraits of Mussolini and other foreign leaders, were also recovered. Nearby, in tunnels and storage depots, the Monuments Men uncovered crates of looted art and cultural property stolen from across Europe — works that had been seized for Hitler's planned "Führermuseum" in Linz.

The search revealed a private world built on confiscation, privilege, and deliberate isolation.

Why the Artifacts Mattered

What the Americans carried down from the mountain —

boxes of papers, reels of film, cases of clothing and art —
became the raw evidence from which the world would later
piece together the story of the Reich's private life. In those
first chaotic months of occupation, each artifact was
assigned a purpose.

Some were destined for law, others for history, and a
few vanished into vast government archives. The
Nuremberg Trials would require proof — not only of
orders and statistics, but of the culture of those who gave
them. The prosecutors needed to show how ideology had
saturated daily life, how the men and women at the top
lived and thought.

But not everything was meant for court.

The Office of Strategic Services (OSS) and later the
U.S. Army's Psychological Warfare Division treated these
artifacts as diagnostic tools. The intimate became legal
evidence: handwriting samples, interior photographs, and
personal notes were pored over for signs of instability or
grandeur. Analysts speculated on Hitler's diet, his
superstition, and his sexual repression; they compared Eva
Braun's decorative taste and diary fragments for insight
into the psychology of devotion. It was the birth of modern
political profiling — the idea that a leader's private life
could reveal the pathology of his public crimes.

The Allied command understood the moral power of
exposure. In 1945 and 1946, newspapers across America
and Britain published descriptions of Hitler's and Eva
Braun's private apartments — the furs, the perfumes, the
silver brushes — contrasting their comfort with the
starvation of Europe.

What had once been private luxury was turned into

public instruction, proof of the hypocrisy of those who had preached sacrifice while living in opulence. Eva's dresses and jewelry became shorthand for moral decay, her vanity a symbol of an entire regime's self-delusion.

Alongside the legal and psychological missions ran another, quieter one: cultural restitution. The Monuments, Fine Arts, and Archives officers traced the origins of artworks and manuscripts stored in the Berchtesgaden area. Their inventories revealed how Hitler and Göring had drawn upon the systematic plunder of Europe's museums and estates to furnish their private world.

Piece by piece, those objects were identified and sent back to their countries of origin, beginning one of the most ambitious acts of art repatriation in history.

The Hairbrush

In Eva's private apartment at the Berghof, the hairbrush sat on her vanity, a finely crafted piece, custom-made and engraved with her initials. It showed clear signs of use— loosened bristles, faint wear marks, and, most importantly, strands of hair.

Captain Paul Baer, an intelligence officer with the U.S. Seventh Army, was the first to survey the room. Like many Allied officers, Baer kept personal items as souvenirs of the defeated regime. He slipped a cosmetic case containing a mirror and a hairbrush, marked with the gold initials "E.B.," into his duffel bag. It would travel back to America with him and remain among other wartime trophies for decades.[3]

Parallel Investigations: Berlin

While American troops combed the alpine stillness of the Berghof, another investigation was unfolding hundreds of miles away, in a shattered city. In Berlin, Soviet forces were conducting their own search — not for artifacts, but for proof of death.

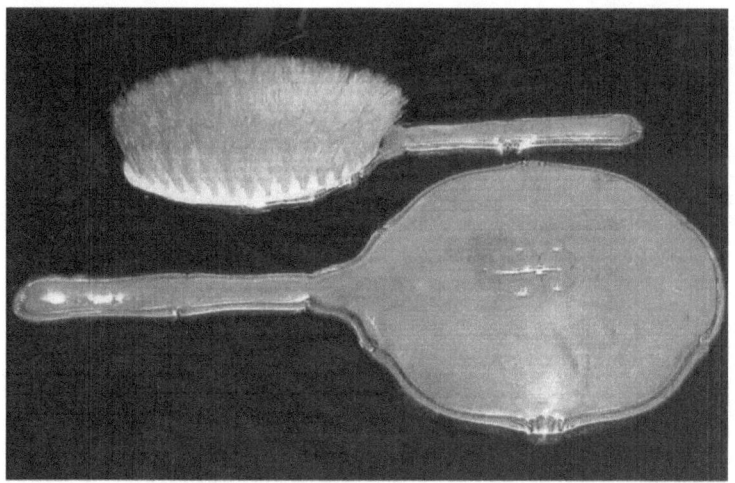

Hairbrush belonging to Eva Braun (The Mirror, 2014, public press image). Mirror Online, 2014.

On May 2, 1945, as the Red Army secured the ruins of the Reich Chancellery, a specialized detachment of SMERSH (the Soviet military counterintelligence agency) began combing the surrounding area. Their mission was clear: find Adolf Hitler, dead or alive, and confirm the fate of his inner circle, including Eva Braun.

Within a few days, soldiers searching the garden behind the Reich Chancellery discovered partially burned remains buried near a shell crater. Nearby lay fragments of jawbones, a bridge of dental work, and scorched fabric resembling a military tunic and a woman's dress.

The remains were transferred to SMERSH headquarters in Buch, outside Berlin, for forensic examination. There, Soviet pathologists compared dental fragments to the records of Hitler's personal dentist, Dr. Hugo Blaschke, and his assistant Käthe Heusermann, who were both later captured and interrogated.

The match was conclusive: the jawbone and bridgework belonged to Adolf Hitler. A smaller, separate set of bones — female, partially burned — was identified as Eva Braun's through the same process.

What They Collected

In addition to the forensic remains, the Soviets also collected charred fragments of uniforms, bloodstained upholstery from the bunker sofa, and remnants of cyanide capsules.

They took the personal effects from the bunker's private rooms — spectacles, correspondence, clothing, and fragments of Hitler's testament – as well as the complete logbooks and diaries of Hitler's staff, later studied by Soviet intelligence analysts.

Eva Braun's possessions in Berlin were far fewer than those at the Berghof. Most of her personal items had already been transferred to Bavaria months earlier; in Berlin, investigators found only traces — scorched shoes, bits of fabric, and melted jewelry. These materials were transferred to Moscow under extreme secrecy and placed in the Soviet State Archives (today RGASPI). They remained classified for decades.

Between the Berghof and Berlin, two investigative trails emerged—one focused on private life and material residue, the other on forensic confirmation. Together, they formed the foundation on which later scientific inquiry would rest.

The Competing Myths

Because Soviet authorities refused to release their findings, uncertainty took hold almost immediately. In the weeks following Germany's surrender, no official confirmation of Adolf Hitler's or Eva Braun's deaths was made public in the East. Rumors spread quickly, fed by silence and contradiction.

At the Potsdam Conference in July 1945, Joseph Stalin told President Harry Truman that he believed Hitler had escaped. Soviet newspapers offered shifting accounts—some claiming Hitler was alive, others insisting his body had been destroyed, still others suggesting a double had been killed in his place. Confusion was not a byproduct of secrecy; it was a strategy.

Western journalists working in occupied Germany found themselves reporting on absence rather than evidence. Without access to Soviet findings, speculation flourished. The mystery hardened into myth.

In response, Western intelligence agencies—the Office of Strategic Services and, later, the Central Intelligence Agency—conducted parallel investigations. They gathered testimony from witnesses who had been present in the Führerbunker during Hitler's final days: his secretary Traudl Junge, valet Heinz Linge, and adjutant Otto Günsche, among others. Their accounts were consistent. Hitler and Eva Braun had taken their lives on April 30, 1945.

Still, without physical proof in Western hands,

uncertainty persisted.

Behind the Iron Curtain, Soviet investigators continued their work in secret. The remains—Hitler's jawbone and partial skull fragment, along with Eva Braun's dental bridge—were periodically exhumed, examined, and reburied between 1945 and 1970. In 1970, under orders from KGB chairman Yuri Andropov, the remaining fragments were cremated, and the ashes were scattered into the Elbe River. The intent was clear: prevent the creation of shrines, relics, or symbols that future extremists might exploit.

Two Investigations, One Impulse

The American and Soviet missions, though separate, were driven by the same impulse: to understand the collapse of Nazi power not only through military conquest but also through material evidence — the physical traces left behind.

In Berchtesgaden, the Americans catalogued domestic life, luxury, and domesticity: silver hairbrushes, silk gowns, home movies, and art. In Berlin, the Soviets catalogued death: jawbones, cyanide, and ashes. Together, these two archives — the Berghof collections in the West and the SMERSH records in the East — would become the foundation of postwar knowledge about Hitler and Eva Braun.

The Historical Residue

By the time both investigations concluded, historians had reconstructed nearly every hour of Hitler's final days and of Eva Braun's final decisions. Yet what lingered most forcefully were the contrasts. In the mountains, Eva's elegant belongings spoke of vanity and denial; in Berlin, her remains told of devotion unto death.

The Fate of the Artifacts

The Berghof's treasures were dispersed into various collections for study. Most items were shipped to collection points in Munich and Wiesbaden, where U.S. Army curators photographed and cataloged them before distributing them to legal, archival, or cultural departments.

Hitler's personal library, several thousand volumes thick, was transferred to the Library of Congress in Washington, where it remains preserved in the Rare Books Division. Eva Braun's photographs and color films — among the first domestic color footage of the Nazi elite — were deposited with the U.S. National Archives and later duplicated for the Bundesarchiv in Germany.

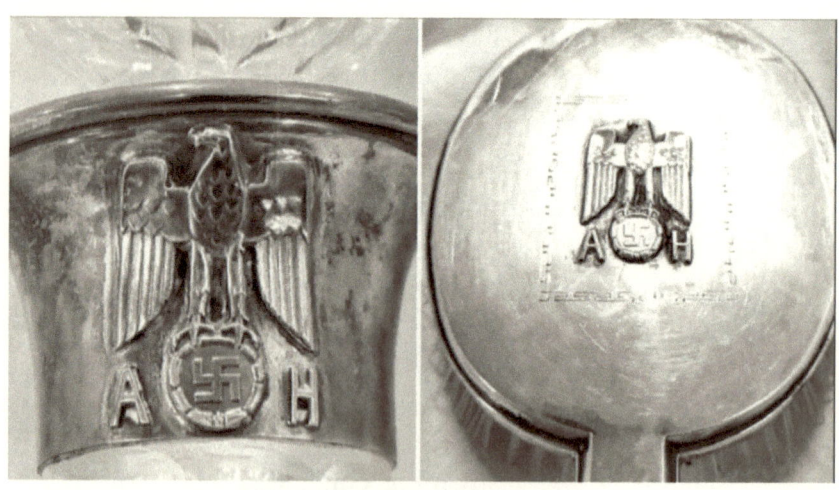

Hitler's Personal Belongings

Legacy of the Search

The Allied investigation was an early exercise in forensic history. Each object, however ordinary, was treated as a fragment of evidence from one of the darkest regimes in modern memory.

By the end of May 1945, the Berghof was sealed. Within months, the compound was demolished by Allied order. Yet what investigators carried down from the mountain that May—films, letters, and personal effects—continued to shape historical understanding long after the walls were gone.

But one artifact would lie hidden for decades. Between its bristles clung dozens of strands of Eva's hair, shed during daily grooming and preserved in the cool, dry air of the Bavarian Alps. Encoded within those fragile filaments lay her complete genetic blueprint—including the markers that would have horrified Nazi leaders had they possessed the means to detect them in 1945.

[1] William I. Hitchcock, The Bitter Road to Freedom: A New History of the Liberation of Europe (New York: Free Press, 2008), 375–377; U.S. Army Center of Military History, The Last Offensive, by Charles B. MacDonald (Washington, D.C.: Government Printing Office, 1973), 456–458; and Robert M. Edsel, The Monuments Men: Allied Heroes, Nazi Thieves, and the Greatest Treasure Hunt in History (New York: Center Street, 2009), 382–385.

[2] U.S. Army Counter Intelligence Corps, Final Report: Activities in the Berchtesgaden–Obersalzberg Area, May–June 1945, Records of the U.S. Army Intelligence Division (Record Group 319), National Archives, College Park, MD; Charles B. MacDonald, The Last Offensive (Washington, D.C.: U.S. Government Printing Office, 1973), 456–458; and Robert M. Edsel with Bret Witter, The Monuments Men: Allied Heroes, Nazi Thieves, and the Greatest Treasure Hunt in History (New York: Center Street, 2009), 383.

[3] AFP, "DNA Shows Eva Braun May Have Had Jewish Ancestry," Times of Israel, April 5, 2014.

Chapter 5—When Blood Became Evidence

———————————◆———————————

IN 1945, NO SCIENTIFIC discipline existed that could
read ancestry from a strand of hair. The transformation of
Eva Braun's hairbrush from an unremarkable personal
object into a piece of genetic evidence took more than sixty
years of scientific progress.

When American serviceman Paul Baer picked up a
simple hairbrush from the Berghof as a souvenir, it was
carried home across the Atlantic with the rest of his gear,
tucked among uniforms, snapshots, and other small
keepsakes from a life-changing campaign. It sat in his
basement, surrounded by old tools, worn shoes, and folded
newspapers, as years turned into decades. Dust gathered,
children grew up and moved away, and new memories
layered over old ones, but the hairbrush remained where he
had left it, silent and untouched in the dark, a forgotten
witness to a past no one in the house talked about anymore.

After Paul Baer died in the 1970s, his son, Alan Baer,
discovered the items and sold the hairbrush to a dealer in
historical relics. It later passed through the antiquities
market and was ultimately acquired by John Reznikoff, a
specialist in historically significant hair and forensic
memorabilia, who documented and preserved the item's
provenance.[1]

The era of forensics would transform brushes and combs
into biological records, carrying evidence not only of
ownership but of origin. The story of Eva Braun, once told

through photographs and memory, was about to be rewritten by her own DNA.

Why Earlier Generations Could Not Know

For most of the twentieth century, ancestry was inferred through documents and oral history: birth records, baptismal registries, marriage certificates, and family lore. These methods were inherently fragile. Records were lost, altered, or deliberately falsified—especially in Central Europe, where borders shifted repeatedly and where religious conversion, forced assimilation, and war disrupted generational continuity.

Nazi racial policy relied on this documentary system. The regime classified people through genealogical charts and paper records, not biology. "Jewishness" was defined administratively, not genetically. The irony is essential: the ideology of racial purity depended on tools incapable of testing its own claims.

Biology offered no corrective—yet.

The First Forensic Inquiries

In the decades following the war, forensic science advanced incrementally. In 1945, Soviet pathologists relied on visual identification, dental records, and eyewitness testimony. These methods were sufficient to establish death but could not reveal lineage.

By the 1960s and 1970s, Western historians and forensic pathologists started pushing for independent verification of Hitler's death. Still, it wasn't until the collapse of the Soviet Union that a limited reassessment became possible.

In the 1990s, Russian authorities finally permitted forensic specialists to review the original autopsy documents and retained bone fragments. Radiographic comparison and early molecular tests confirmed that the remains were human and consistent with the original identifications.

These were not ancestry tests. They were proof-of-authenticity exercises—important, but narrow.

German forensic experts undertook parallel studies to authenticate artifacts—bloodstains, skull fragments, and dental remains—held in Russian and German collections. These re-examinations marked a transition from wartime pathology to modern molecular forensics. What had begun in 1945 as a search for proof of death had become a laboratory discipline dedicated to verifying history through biology.

What mattered was not what those tests showed, but what they hinted was coming.

From Autopsy to Ancestry

Each new generation of technology deepened the inquiry. The Soviet doctors could only rely on visual comparison; the postwar German and Russian teams added microscopy, radiography, and chemical analysis. By the early 2000s, the same techniques were being refined for mitochondrial DNA testing, opening the possibility of linking individuals not only to their identities but to their ancestral origins.

These state-sponsored forensic investigations established the scientific lineage that modern geneticists would inherit.

When laboratories in Britain began sequencing DNA from Hitler's and Eva Braun's presumed hair samples decades later, they were following the trail first laid by the Soviet pathologists sifting through the ashes of the Reich Chancellery. The purpose had changed—from proving death to exploring descent—but the impulse was the same: to let evidence, however fragile, speak truth against the distortions of history.

By the end of the 20th century, DNA analysis had advanced sufficiently that genetic information could, in theory, be retrieved from long-preserved hair samples, and, for the first time, genetic material could be extracted and analyzed systematically.

There were limits to the technology. Nuclear DNA—used for complete ancestry profiles—rarely survives in old hair unless the follicle is intact. Most historical samples remained unusable. The science existed, but it was expensive, technically demanding, and prone to contamination. As a result, most preserved biological artifacts stayed untouched. Unless linked to specific legal cases, most historical samples—including those from Nazi leaders—remained untouched, awaiting more advanced tools.

That breakthrough occurred in the early 2000s. Technology had advanced enough to revisit preserved biological artifacts, and hair samples once considered inert could now be tested, cautiously and selectively, under strict contamination controls. These advances opened new possibilities for historical research, enabling scientists to answer questions about ancestry, relationships, and identity that had previously been unanswerable.

What is DNA? The Science Behind the Secret - DNA, Heritage, and History

When we think of solving historical mysteries, we often picture dusty archives and faded photographs. But the most powerful tool in modern historical research isn't found in any library - it's carried in every cell of our bodies. DNA analysis has revolutionized how we uncover the past, one molecule at a time.

DNA (deoxyribonucleic acid) is often called the blueprint of life. Like a biological time capsule, it carries information passed down through generations. Every person inherits half their DNA from each parent, creating a unique genetic signature that can be traced back through time. This signature isn't just about who we are - it's about where we came from.

Think of DNA as a vast book written in just four letters: A, T, C, and G. These letters combine in endless sequences to create our genetic code. While most of this code is similar among all humans, minor variations create the differences we see between individuals and populations. These variations are what make DNA testing possible.

There are three main types of DNA testing: autosomal, mitochondrial, and Y-DNA testing. Autosomal DNA testing examines DNA inherited from both parents and can trace ancestry back 5-7 generations. It's useful for identifying relatively recent family connections and determining ethnic background. It's a genetic family tree that can reveal surprising branches.

The second type, Mitochondrial DNA (mtDNA), is inherited only from the mother and remains virtually unchanged across generations. This makes it invaluable for tracing maternal lineages back hundreds or even thousands of years. Although mutations do occur, their rates are well characterized, allowing scientists to distinguish meaningful population patterns from random variation. Additionally, each cell contains hundreds of mtDNA copies, increasing the likelihood of detection in degraded samples.

In Eva Braun's case, this would prove especially significant.

The last type, Y-DNA, is passed from father to son, tracing only the paternal line.

How DNA Testing Works

The process begins with a small DNA sample - usually from saliva or hair follicles. In historical cases, DNA might come from preserved items like hairbrushes, letters (from licking envelopes), or other personal effects.

In the laboratory, DNA is extracted and purified. Modern sequencing machines read the genetic code, producing vast amounts of data on an individual's genetic makeup. This genetic information is compared with databases of DNA profiles from millions of people worldwide. Sophisticated algorithms identify matches and can calculate probable relationships and ethnic origins.

The DNA Project: Science Meets History

With this technology came new research endeavors. One such effort was a collaboration between the U.S. Forensic Science Service (FSS) and a documentary television series. Backed by universities and historical groups, the research sought to satisfy curiosity about history and to test Nazi racial ideas against current science.[2] Among the materials examined were hair samples attributed to Adolf Hitler and Eva Braun.

Working under strict contamination controls, the research team used mitochondrial DNA (mtDNA) sequencing to analyze genetic material that had survived decades in storage. Their goal was not to sensationalize history but to test how far modern science could go in authenticating biological relics from the past.

What DNA Can—and Cannot—Prove

It's important to pause here and understand what DNA can and cannot reveal.

First, DNA analysis has become a standard tool for ancestry research, not because it is dramatic, but because it is measurable, testable, and replicable. Unlike written records, DNA cannot be forged or edited. Unlike memory, it does not change over time.

Hair follicles are rich sources of DNA, including both nuclear and mitochondrial material. Nuclear DNA in follicles carries ancestry markers from both parents and can identify specific populations. Mitochondrial DNA (mtDNA) is present in the hair shaft, and when preserved under favorable conditions, even decades-old hair can yield genetic information about ancestry, kinship, and inherited traits. It also often survives when nuclear DNA does not.

It also has clear limits: it cannot identify religion, belief, or cultural identity, and it represents only one ancestral line rather than a whole family tree. Mitochondrial DNA (mtDNA) does not tell a story of who someone was: it tells the story of where one maternal line came from.

Modern genetic techniques allow researchers to analyze hundreds of thousands of markers across all 23 chromosome pairs. These markers, collected from populations worldwide, can trace ancestral contributions dating back centuries—distinguishing, for example, Ashkenazi Jewish heritage from Irish Catholic or Scandinavian lineages. The models then assign probabilities rather than absolutes.

mtDNA is passed from a mother to all her children, but only daughters transmit it further, producing a continuous maternal line.

Uncovering the Past, Strand by Strand

The laboratory that ultimately decoded Eva Braun's ancestry was not a flashy television-style facility but a modest academic workspace: sterile benches, clean rooms, and UV-treated hoods. Here, breakthroughs came gradually—through patience, replication, and careful adherence to protocol. The experts assigned to this project were trained to work with these samples and knew how to coax results from fragments damaged by decades of storage and exposure.

A small lock of hair labeled "Eva Braun" was selected for analysis. Although the storage conditions weren't ideal for DNA preservation, the samples were kept relatively cool and dry, slowing degradation and helping preserve mitochondrial DNA fragments. The handling protocol was exacting. Hair samples were sterilized externally to remove surface contamination.

The DNA extraction focused on the hair shaft, where mitochondrial DNA is most likely to survive. The process began with sterile cleaning to remove contaminants, followed by chemical treatments to release genetic material. The strands preserved in the hairbrush contained both nuclear and mtDNA, but at such low levels that sensitive amplification was required for analysis.

Polymerase chain reaction (PCR) techniques were used and then compared against global reference databases to establish ancestral connections. By the early 2000s, these methods had already become standard in forensic and historical DNA analysis.

The process was repeated multiple times using different equipment and protocols. Only when results were consistent across trials could the team be sure they were not seeing contamination or lab errors. In Eva Braun's case, multiple laboratories independently tested and confirmed the results, applying strict contamination controls and negative controls to safeguard against error.

The work was slow, repetitive, and cautious by design. When completed, the mitochondrial DNA provided a clear signal, and it shocked the world.

The Forensic Bombshell

When Eva Braun's mitochondrial DNA was analyzed, her genetic profile revealed that the mitochondrial DNA belonged to haplogroup N1b1—a maternal lineage found overwhelmingly among Ashkenazi Jewish populations and only rarely elsewhere in Europe.[3] The result was verified independently. Controls ruled out contamination. The signal was consistent across tests: the sample was from a woman with Jewish maternal ancestry.

The result was not a vague similarity, but a consistent population-level match.

What the finding showed—and what it did not show—must be stated precisely.

It did not mean Eva Braun practiced Judaism.

It did not mean she identified as Jewish.

It did not rewrite her life story.

It meant something narrower and more devastating to Nazi ideology: In a single test, the language of modern genetics had overturned one of the central dogmas of the Nazi worldview. The woman who had shared Hitler's private life—his "ideal" Aryan companion—carried within her cells the very ancestry his ideology sought to erase; a maternal lineage rooted in the same population the regime defined as biologically incompatible with the Aryan state.

For scientists, it was a striking example of how DNA could illuminate history; for historians, it was a reminder that truth, once buried, can sometimes be found in the smallest surviving strand. What began as a basic grooming tool became a genetic time capsule. Preserved by chance and examined by science, it revealed a lineage that Nazi ideology sought to erase—strand by painstaking strand.

Ashkenazi Jews and Their Genetic Signature

N1b1emerged thousands of years ago in the Near East, likely among post-Ice Age populations along the Levantine corridor. From there, N1b1 moved westward with successive waves of migration through Anatolia, the Balkans, and the Danube basin, reaching Central Europe during the Bronze and Iron Ages.

These Ashkenazi Jewish populations developed a distinctive genetic profile through a combination of shared Near Eastern origins and centuries of relative endogamy after settling in Europe. Geographic concentration, social boundaries, and repeated population bottlenecks shaped a recognizable pattern of genetic markers that persists today.

Today, N1b1 occurs in roughly 10 % of Ashkenazi Jewish women and in smaller proportions among Sephardi Jews and certain Near Eastern and southern European groups. Outside Jewish populations, it is rare, usually less than 1% in general European samples. Because it is so strongly associated with Jewish maternal descent, N1b1 has become one of the benchmark lineages used in studies of Jewish genetic origins and founder effects.

Carriers of N1b1 are not necessarily ethnically Jewish today; the markers do not define belief, culture, or identity. They reflect ancestry—nothing more. Yet their statistical concentration allows researchers to distinguish Ashkenazi maternal lineages from those of surrounding European populations with unusually high reliability.

Over centuries, conversion, migration, and intermarriage introduced Jewish maternal lineages into non-Jewish families and vice versa. What N1b1 marks is not religion, but origin—a maternal ancestor whose lineage traces back to populations long associated with Jewish communities of the Near East and Europe.

Map of Jewish Populations

What the Records Missed

For many modern families, genetic testing has revealed Jewish ancestry absent from family memory or documentary record. Wars, forced conversions, assimilation, and deliberate erasure all contributed to genealogical blind spots—especially in regions repeatedly disrupted by political violence.

Eva Braun's case followed this pattern. No surviving documents identified her as Jewish, nor would Nazi racial investigators have detected such ancestry through paperwork alone. Yet DNA preserved in an ordinary grooming tool revealed a maternal lineage that official records—and Nazi ideology—never accounted for.

What genealogy failed to capture, biology retained.

A Molecular Collapse

The significance of the discovery was not a personal scandal. It was structural.

Eva Braun, Public domain.

Nazi racial ideology depended on the assumption that ancestry could be classified, controlled, and purified through law and documentation. DNA demonstrated the opposite. Biological reality did not conform to bureaucratic categories. Lineage crossed borders, religions, and identities without regard for ideology.

Of course, in truth, Nazi racial policy had no biological foundation, and modern genetics exposed that weakness. Eva Braun's DNA did not contradict history. It contradicted mythology. She was not an anomaly.

[1] "Did Adolf Hitler Marry a Woman of Jewish Descent? DNA Tests Show Eva Braun Associated with Ashkenazi Jews," The Independent (UK), April 5, 2014

[2] Dead Famous DNA, directed by Mark Evans (Channel 4 Television, United Kingdom, April 2014); Forensic Science Service,

Forensic Science Service (FSS), "Mitochondrial DNA Analysis of Hair Samples Attributed to Eva Braun," internal case summary cited in Journal of Forensic Sciences 57, no. 5 (2012): 1265–1268; and Helen Branswell, "DNA Tests Link Hair Found in Hitler's Bunker to Eva Braun," Associated Press, May 2, 2012.

[3] Doron M. Behar et al., "The Matrilineal Ancestry of Ashkenazi Jewry: Portrait of a Recent Founder Event," American Journal of Human Genetics 78, no. 3 (March 2006): 487–497; Doron M. Behar et al., "Counting the Founders: The Matrilineal Genetic Ancestry of the Jewish Diaspora," PLoS ONE 3, no. 4 (2008): e2062; and Martin B. Richards et al., "Tracing European Founder Lineages in the Near East: Haplogroup N1b1 and the Genetic History of Ashkenazi and Sephardi Jews," Human Biology 75, no. 6 (December 2003): 901–927.

Chapter 6—The Shock Heard 'Round The World

---◆---

THE 2009 PUBLICATION OF Eva Braun's DNA results triggered immediate controversy. Some historians questioned the methodology. Others challenged the interpretation. A few dismissed the findings outright, arguing they were too ironic, too politically charged, or too convenient to be credible. The skepticism was predictable. The claim struck at the emotional and symbolic core of twentieth-century history.

To address doubts, the research team released detailed laboratory protocols. These outlined strict contamination-control procedures, including sterile equipment, protective clothing, physically separated workspaces for each stage of analysis, and negative controls designed to detect stray DNA. Given the prominence of the subject and the consequences of error, the safeguards were exhaustive.

Verification did not rely on a single laboratory. Multiple independent facilities analyzed the same samples using different extraction methods, amplification protocols, and sequencing platforms. Each confirmed the presence of the same mitochondrial markers. A documented chain of custody traced the hair samples from their removal from the brush through every stage of testing, allowing outside researchers to audit the process.

While debate over historical implication continues, the scientific finding itself has remained stable: haplogroup N1b1 is one of the most strongly associated maternal lineages found among Ashkenazi Jewish populations, and it

was present in the mitochondrial DNA extracted from Eva
Braun's hair.[1]

Hitler's wife may have been Jewish

4:04pm Apr 6, 2014

Adolf Hitler and Eva Braun

News coverage of the DNA Announcement

One Limitation

One technical limitation that needs to be addressed: the
mitochondrial DNA extracted from Eva Braun's hair has
not been compared with a living, independently verified
maternal relative. This is not because such a comparison
failed, but because no confirmed female-line relatives have
consented to testing.

As a result, critics occasionally describe the finding as
"unverified." This characterization is misleading.

The DNA analysis itself has been verified:

- the hair sample is authenticated as a historical
  artifact recovered from the Berghof,

- its chain of custody is documented,

- the genetic sequencing has been independently replicated, and

- The haplogroup assignment is scientifically secure.

What remains unavailable is an additional, optional layer of corroboration, namely a direct comparison with a living maternal descendant. Such a comparison would strengthen attribution, but its absence does not invalidate the genetic result or undermine the reliability of the haplogroup identification.

In other words, the inability to confirm a female relative does not concern what the DNA shows. It concerns only whether the hair can be corroborated through a second, living source.

The distinction is key. Scientific verification refers to whether a result is reproducible and methodologically sound. Historical attribution refers to whether an artifact can be independently linked to a specific individual through external confirmation. In this case, the science is settled; the attribution rests on archival provenance rather than family comparison.

That gap reflects privacy and consent—not scientific doubt.

What Eva Never Knew

Eva Braun lived her entire life unaware that she carried a maternal lineage rooted in a population the Nazi state defined as biologically incompatible with its own ideology.

Under the racial laws drafted by her partner, that lineage would have placed her outside the protections of the regime and, in theory, subjected her to persecution.

On paper, Eva's family appeared to meet Nazi racial standards without exception. Parish records documented generations of German Catholic ancestors. Births, baptisms, and marriages showed no indication of Jewish identity.

But paper records tell only part of the story.

Across Central Europe, conversion had long served as a survival strategy. For centuries, Jews adopted Christianity to escape persecution, gain economic access, or integrate into surrounding societies. Within a few generations, documentary traces could disappear entirely. Names changed. Religious affiliation shifted. Descendants grew up unaware of earlier identities.

Eva Braun's family fit that historical pattern precisely.

The Braun Family

According to surviving records, the Braun family appeared unimpeachable by Nazi standards. They were German Catholics with documented ancestry stretching back multiple generations. Nothing in the paperwork would have raised suspicion.

To understand how Eva nevertheless carried an Ashkenazi maternal lineage, the investigation must move backward—to Josefa Winbauer, Eva Braun's maternal great-grandmother.

The Kronberger Line[2]

Josefa Winbauer was born in 1851 in Bavaria and married

Franz Kronberger in Munich around 1875. The Kronberger family can be traced through parish records to the Gmunden–Gschwandt region of Upper Austria.

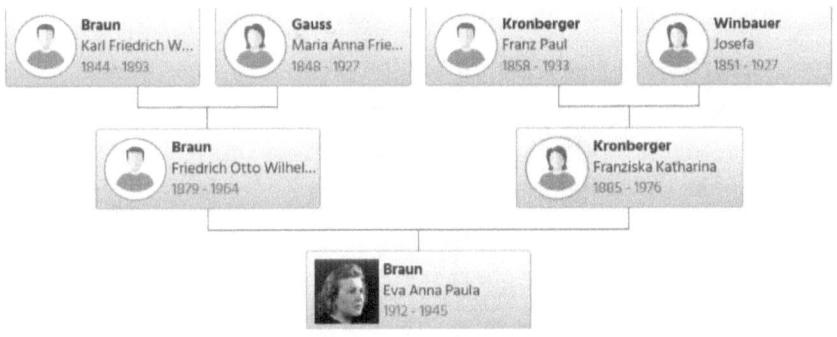

Family Tree of Eva Braun

The name appears consistently in the parish books of Gschwandt by the early eighteenth century. The earliest verifiable entry is Johann Georg Kronberger, born around 1720 and listed as a Bauer or Kleinhäusler—a smallholder farmer. His descendants appear regularly in baptismal and marriage registers, suggesting a stable local presence rather than recent migration.

Through the late eighteenth and early nineteenth centuries, Kronbergers worked as rural artisans and tradesmen, marrying into families with long-established regional surnames. Occupations recorded in church and municipal registers include carpenters, salt carriers, and boatmen—typical livelihoods in a region shaped by forestry, lake transport, and the Hallstatt salt trade.

By the mid-nineteenth century, members of the family moved closer to Gmunden and later crossed into Bavaria. These movements followed economic opportunity, not ideology. After 1860, Austrian–Bavarian borders were porous, and skilled workers moved freely between regions.

By the 1870s, Kronberger households appear in Simbach am Inn. Franziska "Fanny" Kronberger—Eva Braun's mother—was born there in 1885. Her father is described in Bavarian municipal rolls as a Schreiner (joiner or carpenter). Her mother's name is less clear — later sources mention a Theresia Kronberger, née Wimmer, consistent with Gmunden family lines.

By the time of her marriage to Friedrich "Fritz" Braun in 1908, Fanny Kronberger represented the first fully urban generation of her family. She had moved to Munich, worked as a seamstress and shop assistant, and integrated easily into the city's Catholic middle class.

Her upbringing — practical, devout, and socially mobile — was typical of upwardly striving families from provincial Austria who migrated to Munich and Salzburg in the late 19th century.

Nothing in this trajectory would have alarmed Nazi racial investigators.

Which is precisely the point.

Where the Records Go Quiet

The Kronberger line, as preserved in parish books, shows continuity, Catholic affiliation, and social mobility. What it does not show is maternal origin before conversion, name changes prior to parish inclusion, or identities that may have been deliberately obscured generations earlier.

So we must again turn to Fanny's grandmother, Josefa Winbaur, for answers.

Crossroads of Blood and Borders

Upper Austria in the nineteenth century sat at the edge of Europe's Jewish heartlands. To the north lay Bohemia and Moravia, dotted with long-established Jewish communities in Prague, Brno, and Olomouc. To the northeast, Pressburg (modern Bratislava) served as a center of Jewish learning for the Kingdom of Hungary. To the east, Hungary—home to more than half a million Jews by 1900—linked Vienna to the vast Ashkenazi world of Galicia and the Carpathians. And to the south, Slovenia's small but historic Jewish communities traded along the same roads that carried salt, timber, and textiles through Gmunden and Linz.

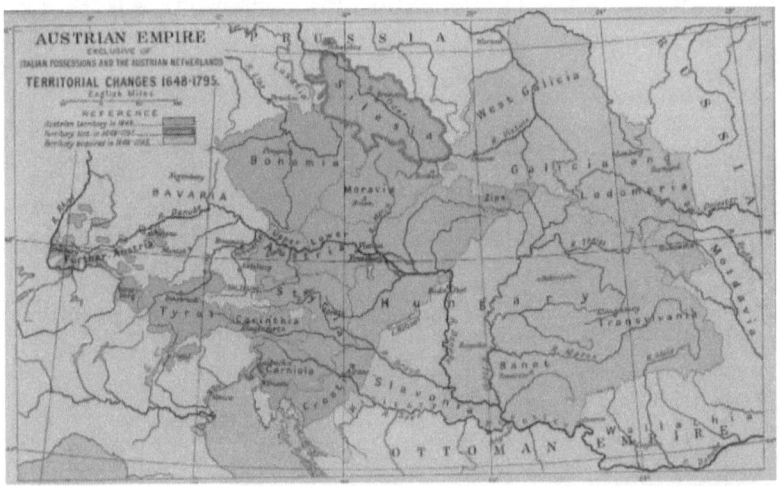

Map of Austrian Empire, 1800

These trade corridors had linked Catholic villages to Jewish merchant networks and migration routes for centuries. Catholic artisans, Jewish traders, and German-speaking clerks lived side by side, sharing dialects, diets, and sometimes bloodlines. Conversion, intermarriage, and assimilation over generations left traces that official records did not preserve. Within this Habsburg ring, religion and ethnicity overlapped more than they divided.

In such a setting, ancestry was not fixed by borders or faith. It was shaped by proximity, mobility, and time. It's easy to imagine how a lineage from Gschwandt or Gmunden, recorded only as "Catholic" in parish books, might quietly carry traces of the Ashkenazi diaspora that flourished just beyond the next mountain pass.

Life Under Habsburg Rule[3]

Josefa Winbauer, Eva Braun's maternal great-grandmother, was born around 1851 in Simbach Inn, in Upper Austria. She grew up in the 1850s–1860s in a conservative Catholic society under the late Habsburg monarchy.

Simbach am Inn – Bahnhof und Postamt, ca. 1910. Public domain.

The Habsburg Empire, stretching from Bohemia to the Balkans, was a mosaic of faiths, yet one faith reigned supreme. The Catholic Church had been the monarchy's partner in governance since the Counter-Reformation. In rural Austria, priests wielded more power than mayors, and the church steeple was the tallest structure in every village. To live outside that world — to be Protestant, Orthodox, or Jewish — meant living on the margins of civic and economic life.

This mattered profoundly for Jewish families.

Tolerance, Control, and Conversion

Empress Maria Theresa (r. 1740–80) saw religious uniformity as essential to order. Jews in her realm were tolerated only as economic agents — traders, moneylenders, suppliers — bound by countless restrictions. They paid special taxes, were confined to certain trades, and they were not allowed to own property or join guilds. Their communities were allowed to exist, but only as separate enclaves under tight regulation.

Her son, the reforming emperor Joseph II, sought to modernize this system. His Edict of Toleration (1781–82) granted Jews limited civil rights: they could attend schools, join certain professions, and no longer had to wear identifying badges. Yet "tolerance" came with strings attached. Jews were required to take German surnames, register with local authorities, and accept German-language education. Conversion to Catholicism brought full equality overnight — the right to own land, enter the civil service, or practice any trade.

For many families hovering on the edge of survival, baptism was a passport into the modern world.

By the time the Kronberger family lived near Gmunden, within a generation, this dynamic was well established.

Conversion—whether motivated by pressure, pragmatism, or conviction—was neither rare nor remarkable. Within a generation or so, descendants of converts were absorbed seamlessly into Catholic society. Parish records made no distinction between old and new believers.

Memory faded. Records stabilized. Ancestry receded into silence.

Portrait of Empress Maria Theresa

The Catholic Revival

By the late nineteenth century, the Habsburg Empire was experiencing a Catholic revival. Waves of popular missions swept through the countryside, urging repentance and piety. Priests held open-air confessions and Marian processions that drew entire villages into public displays of faith. Parish schools drilled children in catechism; guilds and farmers' cooperatives met under crucifixes. Religion was the rhythm of the seasons — Corpus Christi banners in June, Advent candles in December.

Being Catholic was less about doctrine than security. Even after legal equality for Jews was proclaimed in 1867, local prejudice remained. Catholic employers favored Catholic apprentices; Catholics could advance in local military or civic administrations where Jews could not. A Catholic daughter could marry into the growing Bavarian middle class; a Jewish daughter could not.

The safest inheritance a parent could give a child was unquestioned belonging.

Antisemitic agitation in the 1880s and 1890s, particularly in Vienna under Karl Lueger, reinforced the silence. Converts who had long thought their Jewish ancestry forgotten were reminded that in times of turmoil, lineage could be revived as an accusation. Discretion became inheritance.

In this atmosphere of outward piety and inward caution, a family like the Winbauers could pass within two or three generations from uncertain origins to unquestioned Catholic respectability.

By the time Franziska "Fanny" Kronberger married Fritz Braun in Munich in 1908, her mother's Austrian village world had already receded into memory.

The empire itself would dissolve a decade later, but its moral geography — its insistence on belonging, its quiet pressure to conform — had done its work. The Jewishness of some distant maternal ancestor, if ever acknowledged, was long buried beneath the rituals of the Church. Only the unbroken chain of mitochondrial inheritance would remember, waiting more than a century for science to give it voice again.

The Genetic Trace That Survived

Against this historical backdrop, the presence of mitochondrial haplogroup N1b1 in Eva Braun's DNA does not contradict the documented history of her family. It explains its silences.

Within the Habsburg Empire, Jews moved between Vienna, Prague, Budapest, and Kraków as merchants, professionals, and civil servants. Conversion introduced Jewish maternal lineages into Christian families. Over centuries, religion changed. People forgot. Mitochondrial inheritance did not.

Eva Braun, Bundesarchiv, Bild 146-1978-086-03. Public domain.

[1] Angela Lambert, The Lost Life of Eva Braun (New York: St. Martin's Press, 2006), 31–33. Describes Fanny's provincial upbringing and her family's move from Upper Austria into Bavaria in the late 19th century. Diözesanarchiv Linz, Pfarramt Gschwandt (Dekanat Gmunden) parish records, baptismal and marriage entries, 1720–1890. Lists multiple Kronberger families (Johann Georg, Josef, Theresia Wimmer), confirming long-term residence in the area. Standesamt Simbach am Inn, municipal rolls (1875–1890), entries for Kronberger household.

[2] Heike B. Görtemaker, Eva Braun: Life with Hitler (New York: Knopf, 2011), 12–13. Notes Fanny Braun's birth in Simbach am Inn and her roots in a "working-class Austrian Catholic family from Gmunden." Angela Lambert, The Lost Life of Eva Braun (New York: St. Martin's Press, 2006), 31–33. Describes Fanny's provincial upbringing and her family's move from Upper Austria into Bavaria in the late 19th century. Diözesanarchiv Linz, Pfarramt Gschwandt (Dekanat Gmunden) parish records, baptismal and marriage entries, 1720–1890. Lists multiple Kronberger families (Johann Georg, Josef, Theresia Wimmer), confirming long-term residence in the area. Standesamt Simbach am Inn, municipal rolls (1875–1890), entries for Kronberger household.

[3] Research by Martin B. Richards et al. (Human Biology 2003) and Doron M. Behar et al. (AJHG 2006) identified N1b1 as one of the key haplogroups that defines the Ashkenazi maternal gene pool.

Chapter 7—The Men Who Failed Their Own Tests

---❖---

THEY BUILT A STATE on the myth of blood and lineage. Birth registers. Baptismal records. Marriage books. Grandparents' names copied into files. Priests and mayors pressed into service as gatekeepers. The Nazi regime did not merely persecute Jews and other targeted groups; it claimed it was doing so on scientific grounds. It promised a new order built on measurable purity.

But the purity was never measurable. It was bureaucratic.

The Reich's system depended on paper because paper could be managed: denied, altered, or destroyed. A file could be "corrected." A record could be declared missing. A grandmother could be relabeled. The state could decide what counted as truth.

Eva Braun showed that biology can contradict ideology without drama, without witnesses, without confession. But she wasn't alone.

Because in a continent of migrations, mixed borders, conversions, adoptions, and erased records, the Nazi fantasy of "pure blood" was not just evil—it was impossible. And the men who demanded purity were the least equipped to survive real scrutiny.

The European Problem

Central and Eastern Europe—where many Nazi officials came from or had family roots—were a historical crossroads. Borders changed without people moving.

Populations mixed. Names shifted languages. Churches recorded what they were told. Communities converted under pressure, married across lines, moved to survive, and hid identities when politics turned lethal.

The Nazis responded by pretending none of this mattered. They acted as if ancestry were a clean chain instead of a tangled braid. But the Reich's own obsession created a quiet, constant risk: if purity is the standard, then impurity becomes a weapon.

A whisper about a grandmother. A rumor about a baptism. A question about a missing record. In a regime built on suspicion, the past becomes ammunition.

This is why genealogy became a political instrument inside the Third Reich—not just against Jews, but within the party itself.

The Paper Machine of Purity

By the mid-1930s in Germany, ancestry was no longer private. It became a credential system.

Their bureaucracy treated ancestry like a passport. To marry, join specific organizations, rise in rank, or hold sensitive posts, men were expected to produce genealogical proof. The SS, especially, presented itself as an order of racial guardians and demanded that enlisted men prove "Aryan" ancestry back to 1800 and officers back to 1750.

But even the regime knew its system was fragile. Their methods had two fatal flaws. Records are not reality: they are what survived, what was recorded, and what could be proven on demand. And records are vulnerable to power. When the state wants a different answer, it often gets one.

The Nazi system was designed to classify others. It was not intended to withstand the examination of the examiners. In fact, Jewish ancestry of more than 1,200 of Hitler's soldiers has been documented, including two field marshals and 10 generals. In about 20 cases, soldiers of Jewish heritage were awarded the Knight's Cross, Germany's highest military honor.[1]

Field-Marshal Erhard Milch, second-in-command of the Luftwaffe, had a Jewish father. The man who helped develop the Blitzkrieg, Lt. General Helmut Wilberg, had a Jewish mother, and one of the most successful naval commanders of the war, Vice Admiral Bernhard Rogge, had a Jewish grandmother. All these men were "Aryanized" by Hitler since he concluded their "Aryan" blood was dominating their looks and behavior.[2]

Similarly, Hermann Göring, founder of the Gestapo and one of Hitler's closest allies, came from a family with Central and Eastern European ancestry, extending well beyond the Nordic ideal he publicly extolled. Göring's descendants exhibit the same regional genetic diversity found across German populations—a reminder that the "Aryan" concept was always a social fantasy rather than a biological reality.

Even among lesser Nazi officials, the pattern holds. Postwar family genealogies have occasionally uncovered Jewish, Slavic, or Romani markers within the bloodlines of those who once enforced anti-Semitic laws and purity decrees. The statistical likelihood makes such overlap inevitable: in Central Europe—where Jewish, Slavic, and Germanic communities lived side by side for centuries—true "purity" never existed outside propaganda.

Hermann Goering, Courtesy Animalia Life Club

Case File: Emil Maurice — The Chauffeur Who Didn't Qualify

Emil Maurice belonged to the most intimate category in Hitler's world: the early loyalists who had been there before power, before uniforms became a national language, before the SS grew into a state within the state. A watchmaker by trade and an early party fighter by temperament, Maurice served as Hitler's first personal chauffeur and moved inside the small, protective circle that formed around him in the movement's violent infancy.

He wasn't simply an employee. He was "old guard."[3]

That status mattered—because by the mid-1930s, the SS was no longer a ragged bodyguard unit. Under Himmler, it was becoming a self-declared racial order. Membership wasn't meant to be ideological alone; it was intended to be biological. SS men were required to document "Aryan" ancestry deep into the past—far beyond what Nazi state law demanded of ordinary Germans.

In 1935, that demand collided with Maurice's genealogy.

When Maurice submitted his ancestry documentation in connection with plans to marry, the SS racial office found a problem that, by Himmler's standards, could not be ignored: Maurice's great-grandfather was Jewish—an ancestry fraction commonly described as "one-eighth." Himmler treated this not as an embarrassment but as a security threat. He concluded that Maurice could not meet SS racial requirements and pressed for his removal, extending his recommendation to members of Maurice's family as well.

This is the moment where Nazi racial ideology reveals its true operating system. The SS claimed to be ruled by principle. But in practice, it was ruled by power.

Hitler personally intervened. In a secret directive dated August 31, 1935, Hitler ordered Himmler to make an exception—allowing Maurice (and, in accounts of the same intervention, his brothers) to remain in the SS under the informal status commonly described as "Honorary Aryan."[4]

The category existed precisely for cases like this: situations where the regime's racial posture threatened to collide with the regime's political priorities. Maurice's story is not important because it is rare. It is important because it is not.

No battlefield chaos. No wartime confusion. No missing documents blamed on bombs. This was peacetime bureaucracy—forms, ancestry charts, a rulebook, a disqualifying ancestor—and then a signature from the top that declared the rules flexible when the right person needed protecting.

If the SS wanted to be seen as the biological conscience of the Reich, Emil Maurice proved it could be overruled in a single afternoon—by the very man whose worldview it claimed to serve.

Case File: Helmuth Wilberg — The Luftwaffe's "Aryanized" Strategist

Helmuth Wilberg was not a marginal figure tucked away in a clerical post. He was one of the Reichswehr's key air theorists—an officer whose experience and doctrine helped shape Germany's modern air strategy long before the Luftwaffe was officially reborn.

By the time Hitler came to power, Wilberg had already spent years building the intellectual scaffolding of German air power: training systems, operational concepts, and the planning culture that later presented itself as inevitable.

That made his ancestry a problem.

Wilberg was born in Berlin in 1880 to a Jewish mother and a non-Jewish father. Under Nazi racial definitions, that heritage placed him in the category the regime stigmatized as a "half-Jew" (a first-degree Mischling). As the Luftwaffe professionalized in the mid-1930s and the Nuremberg Laws codified exclusion, Wilberg's bloodline became an administrative liability—precisely the kind of case Nazi ideology claimed it would resolve with scientific clarity.

But rather than lose Wilberg's expertise, Hermann Göring intervened. The solution was neither scientific nor principled—it was bureaucratic power. Wilberg was granted "Aryan" status on paper, allowing him to remain in service and continue shaping Luftwaffe doctrine even as the state intensified its persecution of Jews and those of Jewish descent. The significance isn't that the regime made an exception. It's what the exception proves.

The Nazis preached ancestry as destiny. Yet when ancestry threatened the competence of a key institution—especially one tied to rearmament and prestige—the regime treated blood as negotiable. "Purity," in practice, was not a biological truth. It was a designation the leadership could revise when it suited them.

If "blood" could be redefined for a Luftwaffe general, how many other careers—especially inside the SS and the party apparatus—were protected by the same sleight of hand?

Case File: First Lady of the Third Reich, Magda Goebbels

Recent archival reporting has revived an uncomfortable question about Magda Goebbels, the regime's most carefully staged "First Lady." Her stepfather—who also formally adopted her—was Richard Friedländer, a Jewish businessman.

In 2016, a residency document located in Berlin archives was reported to describe Friedländer as Magda's father, raising (but not conclusively settling) the possibility that he may have been her biological father rather than only her adoptive one.

What is not in dispute is his fate: Friedländer was deported to Buchenwald in 1938 and died there in February 1939.

Multiple accounts note that Magda did not intervene on his behalf, a silence that underscores the regime's core hypocrisy: blood could be manipulated on paper when useful, but discarded—without hesitation—when inconvenient.

Magda Goebbels, Public Domain

These cases illustrate that racial classification under the Third Reich was primarily a political instrument—rewritten, suspended, or selectively enforced when it served those in power. In the decades that followed, advances in genetic science would turn that system on its head, shifting scrutiny to the men who authored and enforced it—including Adolf Hitler himself.

Case File: Hitler's Haplogroup

Adolf Hitler's own ancestry has been a subject of rampant speculation and intense controversy for more than 80 years.

Rumors had surrounded him for decades: his father, Alois, was born out of wedlock to a young woman named Maria Schickelgruber. Alois' father was allegedly Leopold Frankenberger, a young Jewish man whose family employed Maria as a maid. Years later, she married Johann Georg Hiedler (the name's spelling was later changed to "Hitler"), whose surname her son adopted.

In 2025, the author of Hitler's DNA: Blueprint of a Dictator uncovered a new source of Hitler's DNA: blood extracted from a small piece of fabric cut from the sofa where Hitler shot himself in his Berlin bunker.

The provenance was clear: in the days following his death, the Soviets controlled access to the bunker, and few people were allowed access. Among those who were permitted to enter was Lieutenant Colonel Roswell P Rosengren, public information officer for General Dwight D Eisenhower, the Supreme Allied Commander in Europe. While taking various souvenirs, Rosengren cut out a swatch of the fabric on the sofa on which Hitler had shot himself – and which, crucially, was stained with blood.

He took it home to the United States and kept it under lock and key before passing it down to his son. It was later acquired by the Gettysburg Museum of History in Pennsylvania, which, in turn, offered it for DNA analysis. Accompanying the swatch was a signed affidavit from Rosengren's son confirming its provenance.

The sample was then submitted for identification. In cases like this, it is standard practice to analyze the DNA from the sample and compare it with either a previously authenticated sample from the individual in question or the DNA of a close relative. DNA was obtained from a distant relative who consented to testing.

The result was conclusive: The blood sample, and thus the DNA in it, belonged to Hitler.[5]

The resulting dominant paternal haplogroup identified was E1b1b (also known as E-M35 or one of its subclades).[6]

E1b1b is relatively uncommon in northern and western Europe but occurs at much higher frequencies in populations of North Africa and the eastern Mediterranean. Geneticists have long identified it as a major lineage among Berber-speaking populations of the Maghreb and as one of several founding paternal lineages present in Jewish populations, including both Ashkenazi and Sephardic groups. Its presence does not imply recent ancestry from any single population. Still, it does firmly situate a paternal line within broader Near Eastern and Mediterranean population history rather than an exclusively "Germanic" one.

These findings did not demonstrate that Hitler himself had Jewish ancestry, nor did they resolve longstanding rumors about his family origins. What they did undermine—quietly but decisively—was the biological absolutism at the core of Nazi racial ideology. The man who presided over a regime obsessed with blood purity and ancestral classification appears, through the tools of modern genetics, to have belonged to the very continuum of mixed human populations that his ideology denied.

The piece of fabric held in the Gettysburg Museum of History closely matched photographs of the blood-stained sofa in Hitler's Berlin bunker. (Photo by Shutterstock)

[1] Bryan Mark Rigg, Hitler's Jewish Soldiers: The Untold Story of Nazi Racial Laws and Men of Jewish Descent in the German Military (Lawrence: University Press of Kansas, 2002)

[2] Ibid

[3] Peter Hoffmann, Hitler's Personal Security: Protecting the Führer, 1921–1945 (New York: Da Capo Press, 2000), 50–51.

[4] Roderick Stackelberg, Hitler's Germany: Origins, Interpretations, Legacies (London: Routledge, 2002), 116.

[5] Jimmy So, "DNA Tests: Hitler Descended From Jews, Africans?" CBS News, August 25, 2010; "Der Führer's secret past," Maclean's, September 9, 2010

[6] "Hitler Likely Had Jewish, African Roots, Daily Mail Says," Bloomberg, August 24, 2010 accessed December 19, 2025.

Chapter 8—The End Of Racial Mythology

❖

THE DISCOVERY THAT EVA Braun had Jewish ancestry is more than just a historical curiosity. It changes our view of the Nazi inner circle, exposes the complete failure of racial science, and provides a powerful perspective to understand the irrational basis of hatred tied to ancestry.

When scientists confirmed that Hitler's partner carried the very genetic markers his regime aimed to erase, they did more than point out historical irony—they revealed lasting truths about identity, prejudice, and human genetics that continue to influence how we think about race today.

Modern DNA continues to shatter illusions about race, ancestry, and identity. Eva's case shows that categories used to divide people are often based on incomplete data, false assumptions, or deliberate lies that persist for centuries. Only modern genetics can peel away these illusions, revealing truths that history alone could never fully uncover.

Rewriting History One Test at a Time

Genetic testing has already transformed how people and societies understand ancestry. Millions of individuals have uncovered surprising roots—religions their families once rejected, groups they never knew were part of, and geographic origins that challenge family stories—altering both personal histories and broader historical perspectives.

When science examined the question of Thomas Jefferson and Sally Hemings, it upended two centuries of denial.

Rumors had circulated for decades that Jefferson and Hemings had not only maintained an intimate relationship but that he had fathered children with the enslaved woman. For generations, Jefferson's descendants wholly denied the idea, claiming the rumors were unfounded and false.

But DNA testing in 1998 proved otherwise, confirming that the Jefferson male line was indeed linked to Hemings's descendants.[1] What had been dismissed as rumor became documented history—forcing Americans to face the contradictions between liberty and bondage within the nation's founding story.

Illustration of Jefferson and Hemings

Across the Atlantic, DNA has revealed another buried past. Studies of Iberian and Latin American populations show that as many as one in five carry Sephardic Jewish markers—evidence of families who converted, often under duress, during the Spanish Inquisition. Many of these conversos adopted Christian names, outwardly practicing Catholicism while secretly observing Jewish rites: lighting candles in hidden corners, whispering prayers in Latin or Spanish, passing down traces of memory as ritual rather than genealogy. Over time, fear did what fire and edict could not—it erased lineage from public memory.

Yet the genetic record endures. Modern descendants, upon learning of their Sephardic heritage, often describe a haunting sense of recognition—a continuity that survived where archives did not.

Even in the far North, DNA has redrawn the edges of history. In Iceland, a handful of individuals were found to carry mitochondrial DNA of Native American origin, a maternal signature inherited through an unbroken line of mothers.

The discovery suggested that Norse explorers who sailed to North America around the year 1000—described in sagas as encounters with the "Skrælings"—may have brought back Indigenous women whose descendants quietly merged into Iceland's population.

This fragment of DNA, passed from mother to child for a thousand years, offers tangible proof that the Atlantic was bridged long before Columbus, and that history's forgotten travelers left traces not in chronicles but in chromosomes.

Each revelation tells the same story in a different key: what we believe about our past is not always what our blood remembers.

Echoes Through Time

Eva's story prompts us to reconsider how Nazi racial classification actually operated and what other family secrets may still be hidden.

Many people with Jewish roots lived through the Nazi era unnoticed, their lives spared by luck, incomplete paperwork, or a local official's interpretation of a file. Some survived because a grandparent's background was unknown or misrecorded; others were exposed because a neighbor talked, a document surfaced, or a rumor reached the wrong ears.

This makes the system's supposed "science" look frighteningly fragile. Lives could turn on a maiden name, a whispered story, or a missing birth certificate, rather than any clear or consistent rule.

Eva's case, and the DNA evidence that complicates her place in Hitler's inner circle, underlines how much depended on flawed assumptions and accidents of documentation. It shows that behind the rigid language of "blood" and "race" were messy, overlapping family histories—and that the difference between safety and destruction was often terrifyingly random.

[1] Thomas Jefferson Foundation, "Monticello Affirms Thomas Jefferson Fathered Children with Sally Hemings," updated June 6, 2018, https://www.monticello.org/slavery/jefferson-slavery/thomas-jefferson-and-sally-hemings-a-brief-account/monticello-affirms-thomas-jefferson-fathered-children-with-sally-hemings/

Closing Thoughts

The Third Reich collapsed in 1945. Its racial mythology did not. Variations of it have resurfaced repeatedly—refashioned, renamed, and repackaged—each time claiming new authority and insisting that identity can be reduced to blood alone.

When science revealed that Hitler's wife carried the very genetic heritage his regime sought to erase, they exposed the bankruptcy of racial ideology itself. The claim of genetic purity and superiority collapsed the moment it encountered scientific truth.

The discovery shows how even the most confident assumptions about ancestry can be entirely wrong, despite generations of family tradition, official documentation, and exhaustive investigations. The Nazi regime devoted immense resources to rooting out Jewish heritage—training genealogists, scrutinizing millions of documents, and inventing pseudo-scientific methods to detect "racial" traits. Yet all of this failed to uncover the Jewish ancestry of the woman closest to Hitler, the supposed embodiment of Aryan purity.

This was not just a minor oversight but a clear example of why racial categories disintegrate under scientific examination. DNA analysis has shown that physical traits once used to categorize humans by race are unrelated to intelligence, morality, or worth. The boundaries created to justify centuries of discrimination and violence are not biological truths but social inventions.

Modern genetics has debunked every core claim of racial ideology, demonstrating that hatred based on ancestry is rooted in ignorance, not science.

DNA serves as the ultimate truth-teller in a world where propaganda, pride, and prejudice often cloud reality. Unlike oral tradition or forged documents, the genetic code contained in every cell provides an unchangeable record of ancestral journeys—a record that remains intact regardless of denial or distortion.

Recognizing the power of genetic truth means accepting that DNA analysis can uncover secrets once believed to be permanently hidden, challenge long-standing assumptions, and reveal connections that contradict entire family stories.

History is often preserved by those who control the record. Biology persists without their permission.

Note from the Author

This book is not an argument about belief, identity, or moral worth. It is an examination of evidence—and of what happens when evidence is finally allowed to speak in a system built to silence it.

The Third Reich presented its racial ideology as scientific, inevitable, and absolute. In reality, it relied on paperwork, assumptions, and enforced ignorance. Ancestry was declared, not tested. Categories were imposed, not examined. The system functioned only because the tools to challenge it did not yet exist—or were deliberately forbidden.

Modern genetics does not retroactively judge the past. It does something quieter and more disruptive: it measures. DNA does not confirm ideology, and it does not align with political necessity. It records inheritance without regard for borders, religion, or law. When applied carefully and responsibly, it exposes the distance between myth and biology.

In writing this book, I have been deliberate about restraint. DNA evidence has limits. It cannot define culture, belief, or lived experience. It cannot deliver absolute certainty, only probabilities grounded in population data and replication. Where claims remain contested, they are treated as such. Where attribution depends on archival provenance rather than living comparison, that distinction is made explicit.

Eva Braun's DNA does not redefine her life, nor does it retroactively assign identity. It matters because it reveals how fragile the regime's claims always were—and how close to the center of power those contradictions could exist without detection. The same is true of the Nazi officials examined in these pages. Their stories are not included for scandal, but for structure: they show how racial ideology collapsed whenever it encountered reality.

This work relies on a wide range of sources: archival records, peer-reviewed genetic studies, forensic reports, and established historical scholarship. Where interpretation enters, it is separated from evidence. Where evidence is incomplete, uncertainty is acknowledged rather than filled with speculation.

Biology does not care what a state demands. It remembers what history often forgets. That, ultimately, is what endures.

If this book offered new insights or challenged assumptions, a brief Amazon review helps others discover it. Reviews are one of the most essential ways for readers to support independent works.

Thank you.

The full catalog of books by Anthony Brewer and Unbound Press can be found at www.unboundpressbooks.com.

More books by Anthony Brewer:

(Coming soon)

Ancient Society for the DNA Age. (Based on Lewis Henry Morgan)

Primitive Culture Revisited - What Tylor Got Right—and Wrong—About Human Origins. (Based on Edward Tylor)

Approach to Interpretation

Where the sources differ—as they sometimes do between emigrant accounts and tribal oral histories—this book acknowledges those discrepancies rather than smoothing them over. The goal is not to impose a single perspective but to present a fuller, more honest picture of frontier life by foregrounding women's voices across cultures.

Transparency and Documentation

Endnotes provide direct citations for quotations, events, and data. To maintain readability for general audiences while preserving academic rigor, sources are consolidated in the notes rather than interrupting the narrative.
Every effort has been made to use verifiable, documented, and scholarly-supported materials. No anecdote or quote is included unless it can be tied to a traceable primary or secondary source.

Notes on Sources

This book synthesizes material from:

- Published German and English-language biographies
- Archival records and documented statements
- Genealogical and demographic research
- Academic analysis or identity, race theory, and personal histories in Nazi Germany

All interpretations are original contextual readings grounded in established documentary sources, conflicting accounts, and gaps in the historical record.

About the Author

Anthony Brewer is a lifelong history and genealogy enthusiast with a deep passion for uncovering the stories that connect families across generations. Coming from a proud military family with service spanning multiple generations, including World War II, Anthony's background instilled in him an appreciation for heritage, sacrifice, and enduring family ties.

With Austrian, German, and Ashkenazi roots, Anthony has long been fascinated by the genetics of Central Europe and the cultural histories of its people. His expertise extends beyond traditional research—he has guided countless individuals in interpreting their DNA results, revealing hidden ancestry, and making sense of the legacies that shaped their families.

Anthony is dedicated to transforming genealogical discoveries into meaningful narratives, keepsakes, and books that preserve memory for future generations. His work blends rigorous research with a storyteller's touch, ensuring that family histories are not only recorded but also celebrated.

Appendix

The same genetic revolution that revealed Eva Braun's hidden ancestry is now accessible to anyone with a simple DNA test kit. What once took months of careful analysis of sixty-year-old hair samples can now be done in weeks with a saliva vial.

Every person holds within their DNA the potential for discoveries that challenge assumptions, overturn family stories, and reveal ancestries long hidden by history. Your genetic code is a molecular record, preserving unseen signatures of migrations, connections, and identities—even when memory, documents, and tradition have been lost.

What often starts as a search for personal identity grows into something bigger: an acknowledgment of our shared humanity. Every strand of DNA contains echoes of migrations, struggles, and choices that have shaped not only individual families but the entire human story.

As you begin your own journey into genetic discovery, remember that the value lies not only in the answers you find but in the questions you are moved to ask—the curiosity to explore, the courage to face surprising truths, and the compassion to honor those who came before. Ultimately, DNA does not just reveal where we come from. It illuminates how deeply and irrevocably connected we all are to one another.

How Genetic Ancestry Is Determined

Identifying ethnic and religious ancestry through DNA involves examining thousands of variants that have accumulated in populations over centuries of relative isolation. These variants create molecular "signatures" that function like biological fingerprints. Modern algorithms compare your profile against global reference databases—now including millions of individuals—to estimate ancestry proportions and connect you to specific populations, from Ashkenazi Jews to Irish Catholics, Basque peoples, or Native American tribes.

As these reference datasets grow, accuracy improves, enabling genetic analysis to identify connections at levels of detail that were thought impossible just a generation ago.

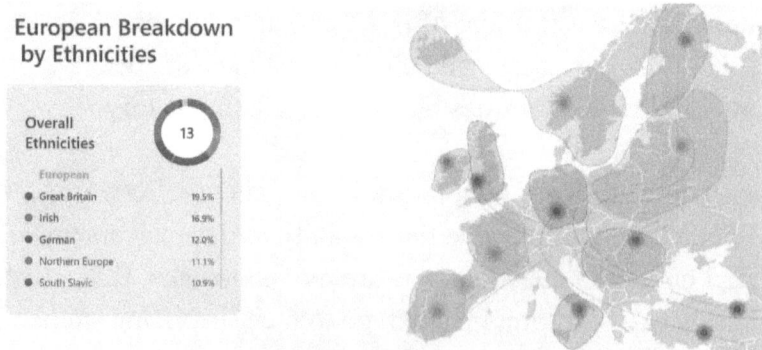

Sample Ancestry Map Results, Genomelink.com

The Frequency of Hidden Ancestry

Approximately one in three people who undergo comprehensive ancestry testing discover results that challenge family records or oral history. These surprises often include Jewish, African, Indigenous, or other ancestries that have never been recognized in family traditions. Such revelations are not confined to families with incomplete genealogies—they occur just as frequently in households with seemingly simple histories.

Biology vs. Identity

It is crucial to differentiate between genetic heritage and cultural identity. DNA reveals where ancestors originated from, but it does not determine the religion, traditions, or values your family passed down. Cultural memory may fade over time, but genetic markers remain, quietly recording lineages that go back hundreds of generations.

Tracing Your Roots: Becoming a Family Detective

Before exploring your DNA results, it's vital to gather as much context as possible from traditional genealogy. A family tree, family stories, and historical records provide the framework that makes genetic data meaningful. By blending genetic evidence with documentary research, you transform raw data into a vivid human story—one that honors both science and lived experience.

Genetic information offers powerful clues, but the information only take shape when connected to documents, oral traditions, and history. DNA should be the beginning of an investigation, not the end. Ancestry estimates and DNA matches generate hypotheses; archival research tests them. Combining the precision of science with the depth of historical sources creates a far fuller picture of your heritage than either approach could provide alone.

Researching the Records

Good family detectives learn to navigate archives, libraries, and online databases to uncover birth and death records, marriage certificates, immigration files, naturalization papers, and military documents. These sources confirm genetic findings and provide insight into the social and geographic context of your ancestors.

Action Step: Gather birth, marriage, immigration, and other official records that trace your family line back as far as possible. Create a detailed family tree that includes dates, locations, religious affiliations, and ethnic identifiers. Look closely at family photographs, documents, and personal belongings for clues—symbols, artifacts, or inscriptions that don't align with the "official" family story.

Migration Patterns and Immigration

Immigration records, ship manifests, and naturalization papers reveal how family lines crossed borders and continents. These movements often explain the diverse ancestry reflected in DNA, while also showing the circumstances that shaped your ancestors' lives.

Action Step: Map your family's migration patterns. Look for unexplained moves, sudden name changes, or gaps in documentation—possible signs that ancestors were escaping persecution or adopting new identities. Patterns of relocation may suggest hidden histories of reinvention or survival.

Ship Manifest Record, Ancestry.com

Studying Historical Context

Tracing ancestry is not just about geography—it's about the cultural, political, and social worlds your ancestors inhabited. Minority communities often faced laws and pressures that motivated concealment or assimilation. Wars, economic upheaval, and social prejudice left genetic traces even when traditions were abandoned.

Action Step: Research the historical conditions of the regions where your ancestors lived. Were there laws or social movements that made ethnic or religious identity dangerous? Interview older relatives for stories about name changes, religious conversions, or sudden relocations—classic indicators of deliberate concealment.

Language and Names

Names and language shifts can be some of the clearest clues to hidden ancestry. Changes in surnames, dialects, or given names often reflect attempts to adapt or to conceal origins.

Action Step: Review your family tree: Do surnames suddenly change without explanation? Do adoptions or "informal" guardianships appear? Such shifts can mark turning points where family identity was redefined.

Military Records

Military service exposed ancestors to travel, settlement, and new relationships outside their original communities. Enlistment files, service records, and pensions often contain overlooked details about origins, affiliations, or unexpected ancestries.

The DNA Revolution in Your Hands

Starting your DNA journey is easier than you might think.
Several trusted companies now offer genetic testing, and
your first step is to choose one that aligns with your goals.
Before ordering, think about how your genetic information
will be used, stored, and shared. Some people test under
pseudonyms or limit data sharing to protect their privacy
while still getting full ancestry results.

Equally important is understanding the types of DNA tests
available and what each can reveal:

1. Autosomal DNA testing gives the broadest
    overview, examining material inherited from all
    ancestral lines. It can identify connections to dozens
    of populations over the past several centuries,
    sometimes detecting ancestry as small as one
    percent.

2. Mitochondrial DNA (mtDNA) testing traces the
    maternal line far back in time, identifying
    haplogroups—genetic "branches" that reveal ethnic
    and geographic heritage preserved for millennia.

3. Y-DNA testing (for men only) follows the direct
    paternal line, providing insights into deep male
    ancestry and connecting men with distant relatives
    who share a common paternal forebear.

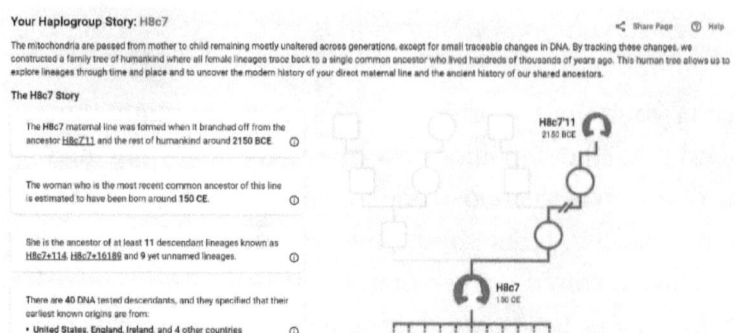

The mitochondria are passed from mother to child remaining mostly unaltered across generations, except for small traceable changes in DNA. By tracking these changes, we constructed a family tree of humankind where all female lineages trace back to a single common ancestor who lived hundreds of thousands of years ago. This human tree allows us to explore lineages through time and place and to uncover the modern history of your direct maternal line and the ancient history of our shared ancestors.

The H8c7 Story

The H8c7 maternal line was formed when it branched off from the ancestor H8c7'11 and the rest of humankind around 2150 BCE ⓘ

The woman who is the most recent common ancestor of this line is estimated to have been born around 150 CE. ⓘ

She is the ancestor of at least 11 descendant lineages known as H8c7+114, H8c7+16189 and 9 yet unnamed lineages. ⓘ

There are 40 DNA tested descendants, and they specified that their earliest known origins are from:
• United States, England, Ireland, and 4 other countries ⓘ

Sample Haplogroup Report, Family Tree DNA

Preparing for Shocking Discoveries

Genetic testing can upend family narratives. You may discover ties to populations with which your family has no cultural connection, or results that contradict long-held traditions or religious beliefs. Such revelations can carry profound emotional weight.

One helpful perspective: DNA reflects biological heritage, not necessarily cultural identity. Your values, traditions, and lived experiences remain intact even when surprising ancestry appears. Still, family dynamics can shift if results uncover hidden lineages, adoption histories, or conversions that earlier generations deliberately concealed.

Action Step: Before testing, discuss expectations with close relatives. Consider how you'll share results, and be prepared for different emotional reactions within your family.

Religious identity can add further complexity. For example, learning of hidden Jewish, Muslim, or Christian ancestry may raise difficult questions about belonging. Understanding how communities view genetic ancestry in relation to faith can help you navigate these situations.

Surprising results may also affect relationships beyond family. Friends, colleagues, or communities may respond differently, particularly if results connect you to groups that have faced prejudice. Deciding in advance what to share—and with whom—keeps you in control of your story.

Begin Your DNA Journey

Action Step: Order a comprehensive DNA test from a reputable company that analyzes hundreds of thousands of markers and compares them against diverse global databases. Choose the level of testing (autosomal, mtDNA, Y-DNA) based on the family lines you most want to explore.

Understanding Your Results

When your results arrive, the real journey begins. Most reports include ancestry percentages, haplogroups, and lists of genetic matches. At first, the charts, maps, and statistics can feel overwhelming — but working step by step turns the data into discovery.

Ancestry Percentages

Start with the big picture. These estimates illustrate how your DNA is connected to various world regions. Remember, these are estimates, not absolutes—algorithms and databases are constantly improving, meaning results may shift over time. Updates can reveal new populations that earlier models missed.

Action Step: Compare percentages with your family records. Are there regions missing—or surprising populations present—that don't match family stories? Use these as starting points for further research.

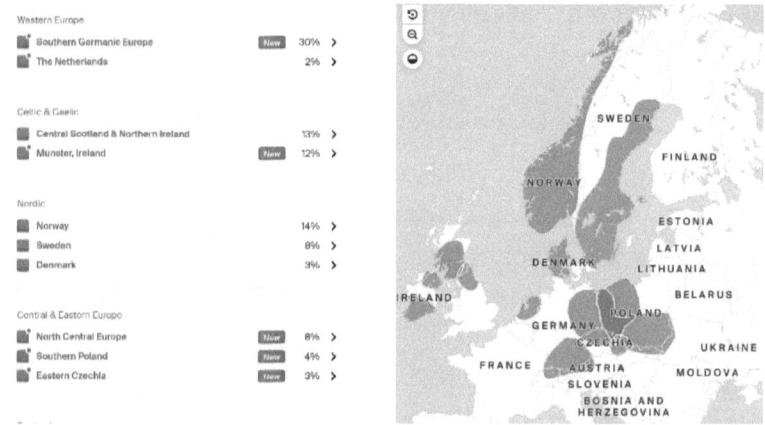

Ancestry Percentages Sample Report, Ancestry.com

Haplogroups

Next, examine your haplogroups. Everyone inherits mtDNA from their mother; men also inherit Y-DNA from their father. These haplogroups trace your direct maternal and paternal lines back thousands of years, revealing ancient migration routes and deep ethnic connections.

Action Step: Note your haplogroup assignments and learn their migration history. Many testing services and online databases offer maps that show how your lineage has evolved over time.

DNA Matches

Perhaps the most practical tool, DNA matching connects you with living relatives who share genetic segments. Close matches typically indicate common ancestors within a few generations.

Action Step: Focus first on your closest matches. Look for patterns—shared ancestors, surnames, or regions—that connect to your family tree. Reach out to matches to compare notes, which can help unlock branches of family history that might otherwise be lost.

Advanced Techniques for Identifying Ancestors

For those who want to dig deeper, chromosome mapping can identify which ancestors contributed specific DNA segments, sometimes tracing back to great-great-grandparents or earlier. This level of precision can pinpoint when different populations entered your family line.

Action Step: Utilize tools such as chromosome browsers (offered by some testing companies or third-party platforms) to assign DNA segments to specific ancestors. Document your findings. Keep a record of ancestry estimates, haplogroup assignments, DNA matches, and how these connect to family stories. Include screenshots, notes, and correspondence so future generations can understand the evidence.

Preserve Evidence for the Future

DNA changes with every generation, meaning your results differ from your siblings', parents', or grandparents'. Preserving genetic material from older relatives— especially those with direct ties to specific ancestral populations—can be invaluable.

Sources of DNA:

- Hairbrushes, combs, razors, and toothbrushes (rich in nuclear and mitochondrial DNA).
- Clothing items, bedding, or pillowcases stored in cool, dry conditions.
- Eyeglasses, watches, or jewelry that accumulate skin cells and oils through daily wear.

Action Step: Store such items in clean, airtight containers in a cool, dark, and dry environment. Keep detailed notes about ownership, use, and storage history to preserve authenticity.

The Takeaway

Genetic testing is no longer the realm of scientists in white coats—it's a tool anyone can use. By preparing thoughtfully, interpreting results step by step, and preserving materials for the future, you become the steward of your family's hidden history.

Book Club Discussion Guide

Opening Questions

1. What was your initial reaction to learning about Eva Braun's Jewish heritage? How did it change your perspective on Nazi Germany's racial ideology?

2. How does this discovery challenge our understanding of history? What does it tell us about the gap between public ideology and private reality?

Historical Context

1. How might this revelation have affected the course of WWII if it had been known at the time? Consider both the German public's reaction and international propaganda value.

2. The book describes how Eva Braun maintained her position despite increasing racial persecution. What does this tell us about power, privilege, and survival in totalitarian regimes?

Scientific & Ethical Considerations

1. What ethical questions arise from using DNA testing to uncover historical secrets? Should there be limits on investigating the genetic heritage of historical figures?

2. How has modern DNA technology changed our ability to verify historical "truths"? What other historical assumptions might be challenged by genetic evidence?

Personal Identity & Society

1. Eva Braun's unknown Jewish heritage raises questions about identity. How do we reconcile who people think they are with scientific evidence about their ancestry?

2. What parallels can we draw between the Nazi obsession with racial purity and modern-day genetic testing for heritage? How have attitudes about "blood" and identity changed?

Contemporary Relevance

1. How does this discovery relate to current discussions about racism, antisemitism, and genetic determinism? What lessons can we learn for today's society?

2. The book reveals how closely guarded secrets can survive for generations. What modern secrets might future historians uncover through advancing technology?

Character & Psychology

1. If Eva Braun knew about her heritage, how might this have affected her relationship with Hitler? If she didn't know, how do we understand her role differently?

2. The book explores various people who might have known this secret. Discuss the moral choices faced by those who kept or revealed sensitive information in Nazi Germany.

Research & Methodology

1. How does the author's combination of traditional historical research and modern DNA analysis strengthen or challenge the book's conclusions?

2. What role does physical evidence (photographs, letters, artifacts) play in supporting or questioning the DNA evidence? How do different types of historical evidence work together?

Modern Implications

1. How might this revelation impact: - Modern neo-Nazi movements? - Holocaust education? - The study of World War II history?

Personal Reflection
1. Has this book changed your view of: - Historical "truth"? - The role of science in historical research?

- The complexity of human nature?

Writing & Narrative

1. How effectively does the author balance scientific evidence with historical narrative? Does the writing style help or hinder your understanding of complex topics?

2. Discuss the author's choice to structure the book as both a historical investigation and a scientific detective story. How does this affect your engagement with the material?

Final Thoughts

1. What do you consider the most significant implication of this historical discovery?

2. How does this book contribute to our understanding of:
- The Holocaust?
- Human behavior under totalitarian regimes?
- The relationship between science and historical truth?

Preview of Women on the Prairie, by Ward McLendon

The following pages include a preview of Women on the Prairie, available at bookstores and online at Amazon.com, Barnes and Noble, and www.unboundpressbooks.com

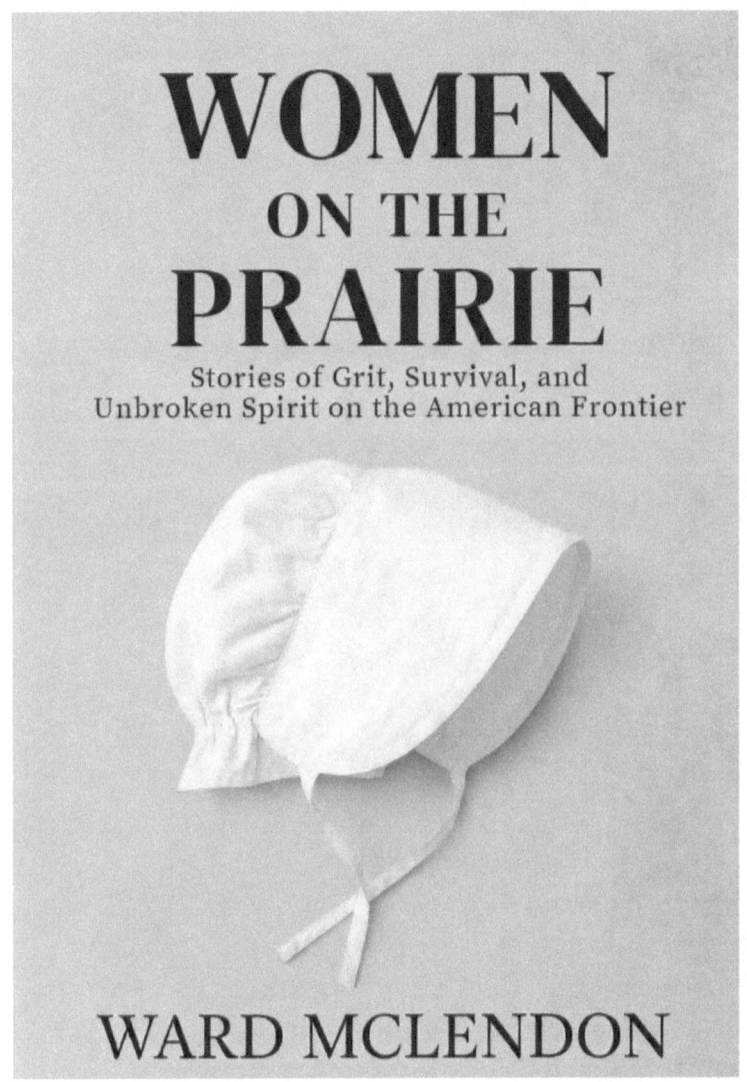

Chapter 1 — Across the Overland Trails: Women and the Great Western Migration

"Courage, my daughters. The West is yet unwon."

—Abigail Scott Duniway

Westward Bound

The land stretched endlessly before her, a sea of prairie grass rippling in the wind like waves on an ocean. Sarah Mitchell stood at the edge of what would become her family's claim—160 acres of possibility and hardship rolled into one. It was 1873, and like thousands of other women, she had just arrived in Nebraska Territory with nothing but a wagon full of belongings, a husband with dreams bigger than his experience, and a determination that would prove more valuable than either.

Sarah was just one of more than 400,000 emigrants who crossed the plains and mountains of North America in one of the largest overland migrations in world history. The Oregon Trail, California Trail, and Mormon Trail spanned thousands of miles, connecting the settled East with the uncertain promise of the West. While men often dominate the popular image of this great migration—driving oxen, scouting ahead, or negotiating with other travelers— women were just as present and vital. Their work, journals, endurance, and emotional labor made the journey possible.

We will explore what the westward trek meant for those women: the physical exhaustion, the emotional strain, the domestic burdens carried across continents, the relationships forged and tested on the trail, and the encounters with Native peoples whose homelands the emigrants crossed.

More than anything, we will examine how the trail transformed women, turning many from sheltered residents of eastern towns and farms into adaptable, resilient pioneers able to survive the harshest environments.

A Journey Few Women Were Prepared For

Most women who stepped onto the Overland Trail had never traveled more than a few miles from home. They had grown up in settled communities: small New England towns with white church steeples, Ohio farmsteads bordered by split-rail fences, and Missouri river settlements crowded with mills and trading posts. Life in these communities followed a familiar rhythm shaped by seasons, neighbors, and predictable routines.

Westward migration was almost never a choice initiated by women. It was usually a decision made by husbands, fathers, or extended families driven by economic pressure, crop failures, rising land prices in the East, or the promise of cheap, fertile acreage waiting beyond the Missouri River. Others were lured by gold in California, religious freedom in Utah, or the belief, fueled by newspapers and land agents, that a family's entire fortune could be remade on the far side of the continent.

The 1840s and 1850s were years of deep instability in the United States. Textile mills in New England closed or reduced wages as industrial centers shifted and markets contracted. Southern and border-state farmers faced declining yields from soil exhaustion, making it harder for families to sustain themselves on worn-out land. The economic depression of 1837 had wiped out savings, shuttered banks, and created a generation of men determined to rebuild their fortunes elsewhere.

Layered over these hardships was the powerful rhetoric of Manifest Destiny, which promised opportunity, abundance, and national purpose to those willing to move west. Missionary societies added their own momentum, sending families westward with the belief that they were carrying education, religion, and "civilization" into new territories.

The discovery of gold in California in 1848 added a powerful new force to the westward movement. News of James Marshall's find at Sutter's Mill spread across the country in 1849, launching the Gold Rush and drawing more than 80,000 "Forty-Niners" toward the Pacific. While most gold seekers were men traveling alone or in small companies, thousands of married men insisted on bringing their families, believing the West promised not just wealth but permanent opportunity.

For many women, the decision involved leaving established homes in Missouri, Illinois, or Indiana to follow husbands pursuing uncertain fortunes. The lure of gold transformed migration routes, increased the number of wagon trains on the Oregon and California Trails, and sped up settlement across the plains. Even families who had no plans to mine often joined the movement, convinced that booming western towns would provide better futures for their children.

Together, these forces pushed thousands of families toward the trails, and women found themselves uprooted not by choice, but by the sweeping economic and ideological currents of their time.

Prairie Bound

The moment they left Independence or St. Joseph, the world changed. The bustling river towns, filled with ferries, blacksmiths, merchants shouting over barrels of flour, and crowds of wagons preparing to depart, were the last reminders of the settled world women knew.

Many emigrants described a moment of stillness as they crossed the Missouri River and watched the last familiar skyline fade. Narcissa Whitman had felt it when she traveled west as a missionary in 1836, writing, "I have left the land of my birth, the home of my childhood… There is no returning." For countless women, this same realization arrived the moment the wheels creaked onto the open prairie.

Once beyond the Missouri, the landscape swallowed them. The trail stretched ahead for nearly 2,000 miles of uncertainty. Women complained of blistering heat on the Kansas prairie, where wagon trains often moved in long, shimmering lines beneath a punishing sun. Amelia Stewart Knight, traveling in 1853 and pregnant for much of the journey, wrote, "I feel faint with the heat and dust. The children cry; the oxen sink in the mud. We press on."

Many women found themselves walking most of the way, sometimes up to fifteen miles a day, because wagon space was reserved for tools, food supplies, and the sick. The monotony of prairie days was broken only by exhaustion, cholera outbreaks, and the nightly scramble to set up camp before darkness fell.

Weather defined the journey as much as geography. Sudden storms ripped canvas covers from wagons, flipped tents, and drenched families to the bone. Lightning was a constant terror on the open plains. One emigrant, Martha Read, recalled in 1852 that a thunderstorm "struck down two oxen and frightened the children so that they clung to me screaming." Women quickly learned to tie down everything that could blow away, including bonnets, bedding, cooking utensils, and to salvage what was left when storms carried half their supplies into ravines.

After storms, the muddy quagmires trapped wagons for hours or days. Women rolled up their skirts, waded into knee-deep muck, and pushed alongside the men because work could not wait for the ground to dry.

River crossings were often the most terrifying moments of the trail. The Kansas, Platte, Green, and Snake rivers all claimed lives. Teams of oxen panicked midstream, wagons tipped, and children slipped away in fast-moving current. In 1845, Nancy Laird watched helplessly as a wagon in her train overturned during a crossing of the Platte: "The water rushed in, and all our goods were carried off. I caught one child by the frock and dragged him up, but we lost so much."

Women also cared for animals during crossings, soothing oxen, holding ropes, gathering scattered supplies, knowing that a lost animal might mean a lost home long before they reached their destination.

As the trail pushed westward, new dangers emerged. The alkaline dust of the high plains burned women's hands and faces, cracked their skin, and irritated their eyes. Water sources became scarce. One diarist wrote, "The water is white as milk and bitter. It burns the tongue."

By the time emigrants reached the Rocky Mountains, the danger changed again: steep climbs, thin air, and snow that could trap a slow-moving wagon train for weeks. Women remembered sleepless nights listening to the wind howl through mountain passes, terrified that the early snows that once doomed the Donner Party might fall again. Even in good weather, the rocky paths shattered wagon wheels and tore shoes, forcing women to go barefoot, their feet bleeding into the dust.

Through it all, women held the emotional center of the wagon train. They buried children quickly when graves had to be dug before wolves arrived. They comforted families whose wagons burned or whose husbands were injured beyond recovery. And while men often scouted ahead or hunted for food, women gathered buffalo chips, cooked meals in windstorms, washed clothes in freezing rivers, and kept small children alive in an environment where one mistake, one moment of wandering, could be fatal.

Their diaries and letters show not only endurance, but transformation. As one woman wrote near the end of her journey, "I am not the same creature who left Missouri.

Hardship has made me capable of more than I ever imagined."

For women, these hardships existed alongside the constant work of caring for children, preparing meals, tending to the sick, and keeping families organized in a world without walls or rest.

Daily Life in a Moving World

Trail life revolved around chores, many of them more exhausting than anything women had done at home: cooking over open fires in wind strong enough to blow sparks into dry grass, washing clothes in icy rivers, and mending worn clothing and wagon covers. Yet women adapted quickly.

Diaries reveal a pattern: within weeks, eastern formal clothing was cut shorter, hems were sewn up, bonnets were reshaped, and sleeves were rolled. The prairie demanded practicality.

Illness, Injury, and Death

Illness was the most feared element of the trail. Cholera swept through wagon trains with terrifying speed, often killing within hours. Women recorded the dread of waking to the groans of neighbors already beyond saving.

Childbirth was another constant danger. Some women gave birth on the trail, in wagons or makeshift tents, then rose the next day to continue traveling. Miriam Davis Collins recalled: "A child was born in camp last night. The mother had hardly rested an hour when the wagons were again rolling."

Others died in childbirth and were buried in unmarked graves beside the long road west. The sound of wheels moving away from the dead became one of the emotional burdens women carried for the rest of their lives.

"She died in the afternoon, and we buried her on the prairie. Her husband drove on with the train," recalled Lucinda Jane Saunders in 1850.

Wagon Train Communities and Women's Roles

Wagon trains were temporary societies: dozens of families thrown together by circumstance, traveling for months in close proximity. Women played vital roles in keeping peace, mediating disputes, caring for unrelated children, and supporting widows whose husbands died along the trail.

When groups dissolved or reorganized, as often happened, women became the emotional anchors that helped families stay connected and safe. These trail communities were complex, but they offered women one unique advantage: the chance to redefine themselves.

Many who had never traveled, never camped, never led groups, or never spoken publicly found themselves cooking for dozens, organizing supplies, negotiating river crossings, and helping make decisions that once belonged solely to men.

Native Encounters: Women's Accounts of Trade, Help, and Cooperation

Popular myth often depicts emigrant–Native encounters as violent or hostile. Women's diaries offer a more nuanced view: many interactions involved trade, help, curiosity, and cautious cooperation. Women frequently focused on Native women: observing their clothing, cradleboards, the speed and skill with which they gathered food, and their family networks. While fear existed, curiosity and observation played a significant role in shaping women's impressions.

In 1853, Amelia Stewart Knight recorded an exchange of berries and roots with a group of Walla Walla women. Knight was initially nervous, but her diary shows admiration for Native women's speed and skill as they traded and gathered food. "Some Indian women came into camp this morning with berries to sell. They soon learned how anxious we were to get them and raised their price."

In 1841, Narcissa Whitman described Nez Perce women approaching her camp to trade woven bags and moccasins for pins, needles, or cloth. She emphasized that these interactions were calm and "more like visiting neighbors than confronting strangers," though communication mostly occurred through gestures.

In the Platte River region, Catherine Sager Pringle recalled Kaw and Otoe women arriving at wagon camps to trade beads, fresh melons, or roasted corn for coffee, tobacco, or cloth scraps. Her diary shows both the cultural gap and the normalcy of these interactions. She noted that Native mothers smiled at her siblings and let emigrant children touch their beadwork.

Sarah Raymond Herndon, traveling in 1865, wrote of Cheyenne women who helped her party retrieve cattle that had bolted during a thunderstorm. They pointed the emigrants toward a creek bend where the animals had run for shelter; in return, the emigrants gave flour and coffee. Herndon noted how the women "laughed at our fright and showed us where the cattle had hid."

Some accounts even record direct aid during moments of danger.

In 1850, Lucinda Saunders described Shoshone women guiding her party to a freshwater spring they would never have found alone, "saving us a long day of thirst and wandering."

These examples illustrate what women on the trail often recorded: encounters ranged from wary to friendly, tense to helpful, but violence was rare. More often, the initial contact was economic—small exchanges, gestures of hospitality, or mutual curiosity that briefly connected two cultures.

But tensions did rise, especially as emigrant numbers grew, grazing lands were damaged, and resources became strained.

Nancy Laird wrote of Lakota riders approaching at full speed near sundown; Helen Carpenter recorded Ute men surrounding her camp and demanding supplies; and Sarah Raymond Herndon described the terror of watching Cheyenne men drive off her party's cattle. "Some of the Cheyennes drove off a number of our cattle. The men saddled their horses and gave chase, but the Indians were soon out of sight. We were frightened almost to death."

Helen Carpenter described a tense moment when Ute men surrounded their camp and demanded tolls, something frequently encountered as they crossed Native homelands.

"A band of Utes came among the wagons, asking for 'tobac' and flour. They would not leave until the captain gave them something. We were greatly alarmed, but no harm was done."

Women documented both acts of kindness and conflicts, providing the most balanced modern accounts of cultural contact along the trail.

Becoming Prairie Women: Transformation on the Road

The Overland Trail was not simply a route to the West: it was a crucible. Women entered the trail as residents of towns and farms. They came out as people who had driven wagons through storms, boiled meals in blizzards, endured the deaths of loved ones, crossed deserts barefoot when shoes wore out, and slept under stars in a world without boundaries.

The trail hardened some, humbled others, and changed all of them.

By the time they reached Oregon, California, or Utah, these women were no longer the same. They were prepared, emotionally, physically, and mentally, for the challenges of frontier life.

Voices from the Prairie: Women's Diaries and Accounts

The most important sources for understanding women's experiences on the Overland Trail are their own words.

Women's diaries were rarely intended for publication. They served as personal records of private thoughts, emotional outlets, or simple logs of mileage and weather. However, because they were unscripted and truthful, they offer the most valuable insights into frontier life.

Sarah Raymond Herndon wrote in 1865, "We are getting rough and hardy. I hardly know myself."

"I am learning to do many things I never thought I could," recalled Amelia Knight in 1853.

These voices help us move beyond myth to discover the truth, not the polished images of Hollywood or the nostalgic stories of later decades, but the real emotional experiences of women who traveled the long westward journey with courage, fear, and determination.

Unbroken Spirit

For generations, frontier stories primarily focused on the male experiences of explorers, scouts, soldiers, farmers, and politicians. Women's accounts add complexity to that view. They show a West that relied on women for survival, stability, and community building.

Sarah Mitchell, the woman we met at the start of this chapter, remained on her Nebraska claim for 43 years. She raised seven children, survived two prairie fires, a drought, and the death of her husband in 1891. She proved up her own homestead claim in 1895, among thousands of women who filed claims in their own names. When she died in 1916, her obituary in the local paper was three paragraphs long and mentioned that she was "a pioneer" and "a good woman." It did not mention the school she helped establish, the dozens of babies she delivered, or the community she helped build from nothing. It doesn't say that she created beauty in harsh surroundings, planted flower gardens in front of sod houses, made curtains from flour sacks, and taught their children to read by candlelight.

The Overland Trail did not simply take people from one place to another. It changed who they were. And nothing shaped the identity of frontier women more than this journey across the continent.

www.ingramcontent.com/pod-product-compliance
Lightning Source LLC
Chambersburg PA
CBHW030302130626
46549CB00002B/657